THE AUTHORS OF THE REJECTED ADDRESSES

REJECTED ADDRESSES
or
THE NEW
THEATRUM POETARUM
with an introduction, notes, and a bibliography
by
ANDREW BOYLE

"Fired that the HOUSE reject him!—'Sdeath, I'll *print* it
And shame the Fools."—POPE.

FOLCROFT LIBRARY EDITIONS / 1974

Library of Congress Cataloging in Publication Data

[Smith, James] 1775-1839.
  Rejected addresses.

  Parodies of contemporary poets by James and Horace Smith; text is that of the 18th ed., 1833.
  Reprint of the 1929 ed. published by Constable, London.
  Bibliography: p.
  1. Parodies. I. Smith, Horatio, 1779-1849. II. Boyle, Andrew, ed. III. Title.
IV. Title: The new Theatrum poetarum.
PR5453.S8 1974   821'.7   74-11000
ISBN 0-8414-3124-8 (lib. bdg.)   Limited 100 Copies

LIMITED 100 COPIES

Manufactured in the United States of America

FOLCROFT LIBRARY EDITIONS
BOX 182 FOLCROFT, PA. 19032

REJECTED ADDRESSES
or
THE NEW
THEATRUM POETARUM
with an introduction, notes, and a bibliography
by
ANDREW BOYLE

" Fired that the House reject him!—'Sdeath, I'll *print* it
And shame the Fools."—Pope.

LONDON
CONSTABLE & COMPANY LTD
1929

*This edition is limited
to one thousand copies*

Printed in Great Britain at
The Westminster Press
411a Harrow Road
London, W9

CONTENTS

EDITOR'S INTRODUCTION	page 1
EDITOR'S NOTE TO PRESENT EDITION	14
PREFACE TO THE FIRST EDITION	15
PREFACE TO THE EIGHTEENTH EDITION	21
ADVERTISEMENT TO THE TWENTY-SECOND EDITION	31

THE REJECTED ADDRESSES:

Loyal Effusion by W. T. F(itzgerald)	37
The Baby's Début by W(illiam) W(ordsworth)	40
An Address Without a Phœnix by " S.T.P."	44
Cui Bono? by Lord B(yron)	46
Hampshire Farmer's Address by W. C(obbett)	51
The Living Lustres by T(homas) M(oore)	56
The Rebuilding by R(obert) S(outhey)	59
Drury's Dirge by " Laura Matilda " (Mrs. Cowley and Mrs. Robinson)	66
A Tale of Drury Lane by W(alter) S(cott)	70
Johnson's Ghost (by Dr. Johnson)	78
The Beautiful Incendiary by the Hon. W. S(pencer)	83
Fire and Ale by M. G. L(ewis)	87
Playhouse Musings by S. T. C(oleridge)	90
Drury Lane Hustings by a Picnic Poet	94
Architectural Atoms translated by Dr. B(usby)	97
Theatrical Alarm-Bell by the editor of the M(orning) P(ost)	105
The Theatre by the Rev. G. C(rabbe)	109

CONTENTS

THE REJECTED ADDRESSES (*continued*)
    Macbeth Travestie ⎫
    Stranger Travestie ⎬ by "Momus Medlar" *page* 116
    George Barnwell ⎭
    Punch's Apotheosis by T(heodore) H(ook)   125
EDITOR'S NOTES   131
BIBLIOGRAPHY   177

LIST OF ILLUSTRATIONS

The Authors of " The Rejected Addresses "
Frontispiece

Lord Holland	*facing page* 1
Samuel Whitbread, M.P.	21
W. T. Fitzgerald	37
William Wordsworth	40
Lord Byron	48
William Cobbett	52
Thomas Moore	56
Robert Southey	60
Mrs. Cowley	66
Mrs. Robinson	68
Walter Scott	70
Dr. Johnson	78
M. G. Lewis	88
S. T. Coleridge	90
Dr. Busby	98
George Crabbe	112
George Colman the Younger	118
Theodore Hook	126
R. W. Elliston	131

Illustrations after George Cruikshank appear on pages 46, 66, 75, 97, 111 and 129.

EDITOR'S INTRODUCTION

ON February 24th, 1809, the Drury Lane Theatre, which had been built with such extravagance only eighteen years before, was burned to the ground through the carelessness of a watchman. Sheridan, who was the principal shareholder, does not, unless he showed extraordinary fortitude, seem to have been seriously disturbed at the disaster. He may have seen, in the destruction of his property, a new development by means of which he might disembarrass himself from his financial entanglements. It was clear, however, that he was not in the position to rebuild the theatre himself, and a Committee was formed for this purpose of which Samuel Whitbread, M.P., a wealthy brewer, was the leading spirit. It was he who dealt alike with the difficult Sheridan and his more difficult creditors. He showed little sympathy with Sheridan's pecuniary embarrassments apart from those involved in the theatre; and Sheridan, who was accustomed to raise money for one purpose and use it for another, was deeply mortified and disgruntled with the brewer. He took his revenge with posterity in a curious fashion (see p. 138).

When the new theatre was nearing completion the question of the opening Address, which it is usual to recite on the first night, was raised. A Sub-Committee of three was formed to deal with the matter, and, unwisely for themselves though fortunately for us, they decided to invite tenders for this article. In this sense a public announcement (see p. 15) was made (Aug. 14th, 1812) in the Press. The *Satirist* (Nov. 1st) thus described

EDITOR'S INTRODUCTION

the Committee. " The Committee of selection consisted of one Peer and two Commoners, one Poet and two Prosers, one Lord and two Brewers. The only points in which they coincided were in being all three parliament men, all three politicians, all three in opposition to the Government of the country. Their names, as we understand, were Vassall Holland, Samuel Whitbread and Harvey Christian Combe." But in spite of sneers and gibes, the Committee were inundated with Addresses from all sorts of names and persons. The form of the invitation deterred the great poets, but the known competitors included such people as Mary Russell Mitford, George Daniel, " Peter Pindar," C. B. Sheridan and, of course, such professional address writers as W. T. Fitzgerald and Dr. Busby. Whether they were alarmed at the number of Addresses they would be obliged to read, or whether they already repented a foolish step, the Committee unwarrantably decided to set aside unread all the Addresses and to apply for one to Lord Byron, then at the height of his fame. This was, of course, unfair to the competitors. " It was," said the *Quarterly Review*, " about as fair as it would be in Messrs. Bish and Carter, after they had disposed of all their lottery tickets, to acquaint the holders that there should be no drawing but that they intended to transfer the £20,000 prize to an acquaintance of their own."

It is known that Lord Holland had recently made the acquaintance of Lord Byron and was a fervent admirer of that poet. He seems to have suggested, in the first place, that Byron should send in an Address in the ordinary way, and there is little doubt that Byron intended to do so. But on mature thought the poet realised (he hints at this in a letter to John Murray)

EDITOR'S INTRODUCTION

that if his Address were sent in anonymously it might well be rejected, a risk his lordship's vanity could not undertake. On being approached again, however, by the despairing Committee, Byron, not without misgivings, agreed to write an Address.

He now set about composing a suitable poem, and it seems to have caused him serious trouble; restless at all times, he was particularly fractious with a composition to be completed in a fixed period and recited in fixed circumstances. Apart from his own alterations, repeatedly ordered and countermanded, the Committee were sensitive and insisted on certain changes; and he, Holland who was intermediary, and Elliston the actor, who had to recite the poem, all seem to have been heartily disgusted before they were done with it. Meanwhile the rumour of the sacrifice of the innocent competitors had been spread abroad. Mr. Ward, the Secretary of the theatre, dropped a hint to the brothers Smith, and the idea of the *Rejected Addresses* was conceived. It had to be developed and carried through within six weeks so as to be ready for the opening of Drury Lane Theatre.

The brothers James and Horace Smith were the sons of Robert Smith, solicitor to the Board of Ordnance; at the time of the publication of the *Rejected Addresses* they were respectively thirty-seven and thirty-three years of age. By profession, James was a solicitor and Horace a stockbroker; but they were privately much connected with theatricals and had contributed parodies and translations to the Press. Some of these were collected from the *Mirror*, after the success of the *Rejected Addresses*, and published as *Horace in London* (1813).

A plan of action was immediately drawn up. They were to produce Addresses as from all the leading poets

EDITOR'S INTRODUCTION

of the day. In spite of the short time at their disposal, and the fact that they were working apart (Horace at Cheltenham and James in London), they put together a slender volume in which were all the known names with two exceptions—Campbell and Rogers. Horace Smith gives his own story of the difficulties in getting the book published (see p. 25). It was published anonymously on Monday, October 12th, two days after the opening of the theatre. Coming as it did in the midst of the discussion of the accepted Address and the protests of those whose Addresses had been rejected, the little book had a rapid and lasting success. Edition followed edition, and in twelve months fourteen editions had been exhausted. The anonymity did not last. It was soon known to be the work of two brothers named Smith. Lord Dudley and Ward, writing to Mrs. Dugald Stewart at the time, wondered whether it might be Sidney and Robert (" Bobus ") Smith, adding, " It would be odd if there were to be two pairs of clever Smiths in the world."

While the immediate success was influenced, no doubt, by the peculiar circumstances and time of publication, the permanent value of the work was immediately acknowledged. Nowadays only the imitations of the greater names such as Wordsworth, Scott, and Byron would be immediately recognised by the general reader; but at the time all the authors satirised were widely read, and the imitations were identified at once. Jeffrey, in the *Edinburgh Review*, wrote: " No reader of Scott, Crabbe, Southey, Wordsworth, Lewis, Moore or Spencer will require the aid even of their initials to recognise them in the portraits." The authors themselves were, for the most part, loud in their admiration; Scott and Byron did not hesitate to testify

EDITOR'S INTRODUCTION

their delight; and if Crabbe and Coleridge were a little sour—as they well might be for their weakest spots had been touched—Spencer and Fitzgerald, who had been most ridiculed, were amiable and good-natured to their satirists. It was, indeed, a disappointment to have been omitted, and it was widely asked why Campbell and Rogers should not have been distinguished by admission. The explanation given by Horace Smith (see p. 23) will scarcely hold water. Mr. Percy Fitzgerald suggests that Rogers the banker was omitted for business reasons, and Campbell the editor for literary ones; but this theory, though ingenious, is unconvincing. The real explanation is surely that both Campbell and Rogers would have been included had there been more time at disposal; but as the authors confess, the book had to be padded out, as it was, with one real address (No. III.), and with other material which was only used because it happened to have been already written or to be easier to write.

While these imaginary *Rejected Addresses* were taking the town by storm, the Accepted Address and the genuine rejected ones were keeping the stage. Byron's Address (given on p. 144) was not well received. The *Morning Chronicle*, on the whole friendly to Byron, said (Oct. 12th): " Mr. Elliston then came forward and delivered the following Prize Address. We cannot boast of the eloquence of the delivery. It was neither graceful nor correctly recited. The merits of the production itself we submit to the criticism of our readers. We cannot suppose it was selected as the most poetical composition of all the scores that were submitted to the Committee. But perhaps by its tenor, by its allusions to the fire, to Garrick, to Siddons and to Sheridan, it was thought most applicable to the occasion notwithstanding its being in parts unmusical and in general tame." On the 14th the same journal, in an appreciation of the *Rejected Addresses*, said, referring to the parodist: " Certainly he has assigned to the pen of Lord Byron a superior poem to that which gained the prize."

It was generally felt that the competitors had been ill-treated; and that the Committee should have kept even its foolish bargain. If Byron's Address had been submitted with the rest and had been honestly chosen as the best, well and good; but it was known that he had disdained to compete (no one was more emphatic than Byron himself on this point); had then received an official invitation, and had finally produced something which was not by any means certainly the best Address available. The *Morning Chronicle* (Oct. 14th) said that it was being inundated with genuine rejected Addresses for publication, and would be glad to see some enterprising bookseller collect them all and publish them, although, to judge from the specimens submitted, English poetry was in no very flourishing condition. The same newspaper, however, praised the lively spirit, varied drollery and easy versification of the elegant volume of pseudo *Rejected Addresses*, which vindicated the age from the imputation cast on it by the prize poem. The *Quarterly Review* spoke in much the same fashion.

Byron was by now in an ecstasy of annoyance and wounded pride. He badgered Holland to make some announcement, and without waiting for compliance himself sent a note to the *Morning Chronicle* (Oct. 17th) signed *Candidus*, explaining that the competitive addresses had been set aside because they were too complimentary to Mr. Whitbread; and that Lord Byron had not been applied to until after September 10th, having previously declined to compete. " *Verax*, a sincere

EDITOR'S INTRODUCTION

admirer of Childe Harold " (apparently Lord Holland himself), pursued the matter. He agreed that it was the duty of the Committee to read the poems. This had been done and some of them were found to be of considerable merit, but for various reasons they were set aside. Lord Byron was then asked to complete an Address he had *projected*. The rejected suitors were at liberty to take their revenge on the Committee by publishing their own Addresses. An indignant competitor, " M.," took up this challenge and demanded whether he and his companions in misfortune were to eke out their Addresses with wide margins and heavy type, or hold a meeting at the London Tavern to collect them?

But in the meantime Dr. Busby (Mus. Doc.) was setting an example to the rejected authors. This individual (of whom a fuller account is given on p. 162) has been criticised as an interloper, but in fact he had a real standing at Drury Lane. He was Elliston's laureate; he wrote most of the Addresses and Prologues for that player, and so had a name and reputation to maintain in the theatre and before the public. But his own poem was so bad as to be distinguished even among so many indifferent ones, and his chance in open competition must have been very small indeed. Nothing could convince him of this. A man so conceited, obtuse, and unabashed was not easily set down, and he contributed the farcical element to the whole absurd affair. He had submitted an Address and the public were going to hear it in spite of the Committee. His campaign against Drury Lane was divided into two assaults —the first was made by his son, George Frederic, and was repulsed; the second by the Doctor himself, and after a brief success died away.

On Wednesday, October 14th, in the interval between

EDITOR'S INTRODUCTION

the first and second plays, a gentleman was seen to stand up in the pit and harangue the audience with great earnestness. In the uproar of cheers and hoots, which greeted his appearance, no one could hear what he was saying, although, to judge from his gesticulations, it was worth hearing. In due course the curtain rose and Mr. Holland (the Assistant Manager) came forward to announce the next piece. He was surprised to find his audience in the possession of a rival speaker. He hesitated, not knowing what to do; but, deciding that his own announcement was merely formal, he made it, in spite of the noise, and retired. The crowd, who were entering into the spirit of the thing, thereupon encouraged the stranger to mount the stage. He did so, and, as is usual in the case of first appearances, was greeted with loud cheers. Mr. Raymond, the Manager, hearing the applause, came from behind the scenes and, at first not perceiving the stranger, who was solemnly bowing his acknowledgments from one side of the stage, took the compliment to himself and began to make his obeisance as well. Suddenly he noticed his rival, and the delighted audience cheered louder than ever to see Mr. Raymond and the stranger gravely saluting each other and speaking, apparently, in dumb show. But the fickle mob soon tired of this, and the cheers and laughter were turned to hoots and hisses. Thereupon Mr. Raymond retired and, as the orator refused his invitation to follow, returned with two Bow Street officers who cut off the stranger as he was retreating across the footlights to the pit, and hustled him off the back of the stage. The second play began but was continually interrupted until the audience were assured that the mysterious stranger had not been ill-treated and was safe. His name was George Frederic Busby. He had

EDITOR'S INTRODUCTION

written an Address himself (see p. 168), but it was sacrificed, apparently, to the vindication of his father whose rejected Address he had vainly attempted to recite.

The next night the formidable Doctor himself arose from the boxes after the first play, and began to state his case. He was Dr. Busby, he said, a lover of the stage, and not ashamed to address an audience in this fashion in such special circumstances. For Lord Byron's talents he had the greatest respect, but his lordship " did not engross in himself all the poetic genius of the country." Not for his own sake alone, but for that of the other suitors, had he taken this unusual method of protest. The Committee had more than one hundred Addresses to select from, and should have kept its bargain to choose one of them. Some were fine—he, himself, had seen two or three that were very fine. Here an interrupter suggested: "Your own and your son's for example!" and this sally was greeted with such an uproar of laughter and cheers that the Doctor could not proceed. Mr. Raymond then came forward to ask that the next piece—a farce, " Turn Out "—should be allowed to begin. Mr. Dowton, the comedian, delighted the audience by improvising the following example of the jealousy of a misjudging world. He had submitted, he said, a number of Addresses to the Committee, and they had all been rejected. He intended, he declared, to go to Drury Lane and recite them himself. Undeterred, the moment the play was over, the dauntless Doctor returned to the attack. He had written an Address for the opening of Drury Lane Theatre, and he only desired his audience to judge between it and the accepted one. At this point he was rudely seized by two Bow Street officers and carried, struggling, from his box to the top of the stairs. He might thus have ignominiously disappeared, but at the last moment he was rescued by the mob and the police were " precipitated," to quote the Doctor's own words, " by the indignant company down the lobby stairs." Borne back in triumph to his box, he concluded his speech, thanked the audience for this " compliment to his poetic genius," and promised them " such a monologue as they had never heard before." Mr. Raymond, for the sake of peace, at last permitted George Frederic again to mount the stage, and the Doctor's address began; but, alas! George Frederic's voice was feeble and amid the noise and laughter it could not be heard. After a short time a candid voice from one of the boxes advised him to go home: " Not a word can be heard from the smallness of your voice, however elegant and large your ideas may be."

The Address was published next day in the *Morning Chronicle*, which added caustically that it was brave and generous of Dr. Busby thus to devote himself, by the printing of his Address, to the justification of the Committee. Byron, still smarting under the criticism of his own Address, seized the opportunity to turn the ridicule upon a more deserving object, and wrote his " Parenthetical Address by Dr. Plagiary, to be recited in an inarticulate voice by his Son" (see p. 166). He sent it to Murray with the request that he should have it inserted anonymously in the *Morning Chronicle*. It appeared October 23rd, but its effect was weakened by the simultaneous publication of a justification by Dr. Busby which at least distracted attention from the parody. This annoyed Byron more than ever, but he seems later to have repented his ferocity and to have made his peace with the Doctor; for his name figures in

EDITOR'S INTRODUCTION

the list of subscribers to Busby's *Lucretius* (published the next year), and he was described by that translator as the poetical ornament of his age.

* * * * *

Reference has earlier been made to the suggestion of the *Morning Chronicle* that some enterprising publisher should collect and issue the genuine Rejected Addresses. The hint did not fall on barren soil. B. McMillan, a small publisher of Covent Garden, advertised for, and collected, the Addresses of the unfortunate competitors from such as had kept copies. These he put together and published (Nov. 1812) in an octavo book (called *Genuine Rejected Addresses*), to which he prefixed the Address of Lord Byron—without the permission, and greatly to the annoyance, of the noble bard. In a well-written preface he alluded to the Busby episode, and paid suitable compliments to the *Rejected Addresses* of the brothers Smith.

The success of the *Rejected Addresses* naturally brought a host of imitations. The first and most impudent of these was a *Sequel to the Rejected Addresses by Another Author*, published by Sherwood (1813). It is frequently found bound with early editions of the *Rejected Addresses*. It parodied the poets omitted by the Brothers Smith—including Campbell and Rogers; although its success was considerable—there were four editions of it—the author's name has not transpired. Then there were the *Rejected Odes* of John Poole and the *Posthumous Parodies* of Horace Twiss, himself one of the rejected competitors, the *Poetic Mirror* of James Hogg and the *Odes and Addresses to Great People* by Thomas Hood and J. H. Reynolds (1825). But for a definite parallel we must pass to a little volume

EDITOR'S INTRODUCTION

entitled *Warreniana*, published (1824) anonymously by W. F. Deacon. In this the same authors are imitated with such skill and wit that the book only suffers because it must be unavoidably contrasted with its unrivalled predecessor. More than thirty years then elapse before we find another notable work of this class. In 1859 there appeared on the occasion of the Burns Centenary a book entitled *Rival Rhymes in Honour of Burns with Curious Illustrative Matter Collected and Edited by Ben Trovato*. It was written by Samuel Lover and, following the plan of the Brothers Smith, it consists of imitations of living authors—Tennyson, Macaulay, Campbell, Longfellow, Barry Cornwall and Thackeray. The prose imitation of the latter is specially good, but the poems must be regarded as parodies, imitations of the form rather than the spirit. Therein lay the genius of the Brothers Smith. In reproducing the very spirit of their authors they were paramount.

It would be difficult and perhaps invidious to try to apportion the merit between the brothers Smith; it has been attempted, however, by at least two writers, and with conflicting results. This is exactly as it should be, for, in truth, the honours are equally divided. The finest imitations, by universal consent, are " A Tale of Drury Lane " (Scott), " The Baby's Debut " (Wordsworth), " *Cui Bono* " (Byron) and " The Theatre " (Crabbe). Of these, James wrote the second and fourth and Horace the first and third (with the exception of one stanza). Of these four, in the opinion not only of the present writer but of other better-qualified judges, the finest is " A Tale of Drury Lane." One's admiration increases with each reading of it, a fact which does much to vindicate the reputation of Horace, often ranked far

EDITOR'S INTRODUCTION

below his wittier brother. It is characteristic that the imitations which caused most resentment—those of Wordsworth, Coleridge and Crabbe—should have been written by James. An acid flavour is also to be found in his notes to the eighteenth edition—a tendency to praise with a damning reservation—which contrasts in a marked fashion with the modest and genial Preface by Horace.

A bibliography of the *Rejected Addresses* is to be found at p. 177. Here it may be stated that the text as altered for the Second Edition holds good. For the Eighteenth (Cruikshank) Edition, which is the text of the present copy, Horace wrote the Preface and James the Notes. These notes have all been faithfully reproduced. Some are highly interesting, some in rather bad taste, and the appearance of the rest is due only to that piety which induces editors of Boswell still to include his note upon " Difficile est proprie communia dicere."

ANDREW BOYLE

EDITOR'S NOTE TO PRESENT EDITION

THE text of *Rejected Addresses* here printed is that of the Eighteenth Edition of 1833—the last edition to be revised by the authors themselves. Horace Smith's Preface to this edition is given, followed by Peter Cunningham's "Advertisement" to the Twenty-second Edition of 1851, written after Horace Smith's death. My own introduction must be regarded as supplementary to these earlier prefaces, for it does not attempt to repeat the facts there set forth.

Of the Notes which are placed at the end of this volume so as not to interfere with the reading of the verse, those originally written by James Smith and Peter Cunningham are distinguished by their initials. For the remainder I am myself responsible.

A. B.

PREFACE TO THE FIRST EDITION

O N the 14th of August, 1812, the following advertisement appeared in most of the daily papers.

" *Rebuilding of Drury Lane Theatre.*

" The Committee are desirous of promoting a free and fair competition for an Address to be spoken upon the opening of the Theatre, which will take place on the 10th of October next. They have therefore thought fit to announce to the public, that they will be glad to receive any such compositions, addressed to their Secretary, at the Treasury Office, in Drury Lane, on or before the 10th of September sealed up; with a distinguishing word, number, or motto on the cover, corresponding with the inscription on a separate sealed paper containing the name of the author, which will not be opened unless containing the name of the successful candidate."

Upon the propriety of this plan, men's minds were, as they usually are upon matters of moment, much divided. Some thought it a fair promise of the future intention of the Committee to abolish that phalanx of authors who usurp the stage, to the exclusion of a large assortment of dramatic talent blushing unseen in the background; while others contended, that the scheme would prevent men of real eminence from descending into an amphitheatre, in which all Grub Street (that is to say, all London and Westminster) would be arrayed against them. The event has proved both parties to be in a degree right and in a degree wrong. One hundred

PREFACE TO THE FIRST EDITION

and twelve addresses have been sent in, each sealed and signed, and mottoed, "as per order," some written by men of great, some by men of little, and some by men of no talent.

Many of the public prints have censured the taste of the Committee, in thus contracting for Addresses, as they would for nails—by the gross; but it is surprising that none should have censured their *temerity*. One hundred and eleven of the Addresses must, of course, be unsuccessful: to each of the authors, thus infallibly classed with the *genus irritabile*, it would be very hard to deny six staunch friends, who consider his the best of all possible addresses, and whose tongues will be as ready to laud him, as to hiss his adversary. These, with the potent aid of the Bard himself, make seven foes per address, and thus will be created seven hundred and seventy seven implacable auditors, prepared to condemn the strains of Apollo himself; a band of adversaries which no prudent manager would think of exasperating.

But leaving the Committee to encounter the responsibility they have incurred, the public have at least to thank them for ascertaining and establishing one point, which might otherwise have admitted of controversy. When it is considered that many amateur writers have been discouraged from becoming competitors, and that few, if any, of the professional authors can afford to write for nothing, and of course have not been candidates for the honorary prize at Drury Lane, we may confidently pronounce, that as far as regards *number*, the present is undoubtedly the Augustan age of English poetry. Whether or not this distinction will be extended to the *quality* of its productions must be decided at the tribunal of posterity, though the natural anxiety of our

PREFACE TO THE FIRST EDITION

authors on this score ought to be considerably diminished when they reflect how few will, in all probability, be had up for judgment.

It is not necessary for the Editor to mention the manner in which he became possessed of this "fair sample of the present state of poetry in Great Britain." It was his first intention to publish the whole, but a little reflection convinced him that, by so doing, he might depress the good without elevating the bad. He has therefore culled what had the appearance of flowers from what possessed the reality of weeds, and is extremely sorry that, in so doing, he has diminished his collection to twenty-one. Those which he has rejected may possibly make their appearance in a separate volume, or they may be admitted as volunteers in the files of some of the newspapers; or at all events they are sure of being received among the awkward squad of the Magazines. In general they bear a close resemblance to each other:—thirty of them contain extravagant compliments to the immortal Wellington, and the indefatigable Whitbread, and as the last mentioned gentleman is said to dislike praise in the exact proportion in which he deserves it, these laudatory writers have probably been only building a wall, against which they might run their own heads.

The Editor here begs leave to advance a few words in behalf of that useful and much abused bird the Phœnix, and in so doing he is biased by no partiality, as he assures the reader he not only never saw one, but (*mirabile dictu!*) never caged one in a simile in the whole course of his life. No less than sixty-nine of the competitors have invoked the aid of this native of Arabia; but as from their manner of using him, after they had caught him, he does not by any means appear to have

PREFACE TO THE FIRST EDITION

been a native of Arabia *Felix*, the Editor has left the proprietors to treat with Mr. Polito, and refused to receive this *rara avis*, or black swan, into the present collection. One exception occurs, in which the admirable treatment of this feathered incombustible, entitles the author to great praise:—that address has been preserved, and in the ensuing pages takes the lead, to which its dignity entitles it.

Perhaps the reason why several of the subjoined productions of the MUSÆ LONDINENSES have failed of selection, may be discovered in their being penned in a metre unusual upon occasions of this sort, and in their not being written with that attention to stage effect, the want of which, like want of manners in the concerns of life, is more prejudicial than a deficiency of talent. There is an art in writing for the Theatre, technically called *touch and go*, which is indispensable when we consider the small quantum of patience, which so motley an assemblage as a London audience can be expected to afford. All the contributors have been very exact in sending their initials and mottoes. Those belonging to the present collection have been carefully preserved, and each has been affixed to its respective poem. The letters that accompanied the Addresses having been honorably destroyed unopened, it is impossible to state the real authors with any certainty, but the ingenious reader, after comparing the initials with the motto, and both with the poem, may form his own conclusions.

The Editor does not anticipate any disapprobation from thus giving publicity to a small portion of the REJECTED ADDRESSES; for unless he is widely mistaken in assigning the respective authors, the fame of each individual is established on much too firm a basis to be

PREFACE TO THE FIRST EDITION

shaken by so trifling and evanescent a publication as the present:

———— neque ego illi detrahere ausim
Hærentem capiti multâ cum laude coronam.

Of the numerous pieces already sent to the Committee for performance, he has only availed himself of three vocal Travesties, which he has selected, not for their merit, but simply for their brevity. Above one hundred spectacles, melodramas, operas and pantomimes have been transmitted, besides the two first acts of one legitimate comedy. Some of these evince considerable smartness of manual dialogue, and several brilliant repartees of chairs, tables, and other inanimate wits; but the authors seem to have forgotten that in the new Drury Lane the audience can hear as well as see. Of late our Theatres have been so constructed, that John Bull has been compelled to have very long ears, or none at all; to keep them dangling about his skull like discarded servants, while his eyes were gazing at pieballs and elephants, or else to stretch them out to an asinine length to catch the congenial sound of braying trumpets. An auricular revolution is, we trust, about to take place, and as many people have been much puzzled to define the meaning of the new æra, of which we have heard so much, we venture to pronounce, that as far as regards Drury Lane Theatre, the new æra means the reign of ears. If the past afford any pledge for the future, we may confidently expect from the Committee of that House, every thing that can be accomplished by the union of taste and assiduity.

Samuel Whitbread Esqr. M.P.

PREFACE TO THE EIGHTEENTH EDITION

IN the present publishing era, when books are like the multitudinous waves of the advancing sea, some of which make no impression whatever upon the sand, while the superficial traces left by others are destined to be perpetually obliterated by their successors, almost as soon as they are found, the authors of the *Rejected Addresses* may well feel flattered, after a lapse of twenty years, and the sale of seventeen large editions, in receiving an application to write a Preface to a new and more handsome impression. In diminution, however, of any overweening vanity which they might be disposed to indulge on this occasion, they cannot but admit the truth of the remark made by a particularly candid and good-natured friend, who kindly reminded them, that if their little work has hitherto floated upon the stream of time, while so many others of much greater weight and value have sunk to rise no more, it has been solely indebted for its buoyancy to that specific levity which enables feathers, straws, and similar trifles to defer their submersion until they have become thoroughly saturated with the waters of oblivion, when they quickly meet the fate which they had long before merited.

Our ingenuous and ingenious friend furthermore observed, that the demolition of Drury Lane Theatre by fire, its reconstruction under the auspices of the celebrated Mr. Whitbread,[1] the reward offered by the

[1] Samuel Whitbread, M.P. He died by his own hand in 1815. P.C.

PREFACE TO THE EIGHTEENTH EDITION

Committee for an opening address, and the public recitation of a poem composed expressly for the occasion by Lord Byron, one of the most popular writers of the age, formed an extraordinary concurrence of circumstances which could not fail to insure the success of the *Rejected Addresses*, while it has subsequently served to fix them in the memory of the public, so far at least as a poor immortality of twenty years can be said to have effected that object. In fact, continued our impartial and affectionate monitor, your little work owes its present obscure existence entirely to the accidents that have surrounded and embalmed it—even as flies, and other worthless insects, may long survive their natural date of extinction, if they chance to be preserved in amber, or any similar substance.

> The things, we know, are neither rich nor rare—
> We wonder how the devil they got there!

With the natural affection of parents for the offspring of their own brains, we ventured to hint that some portion of our success might perhaps be attributable to the manner in which the different imitations were executed; but our worthy friend protested that his sincere regard for us, as well as for the cause of truth, compelled him to reject our claim, and to pronounce that, when once the idea had been conceived, all the rest followed as a matter of course, and might have been executed by any other hands not less felicitously than by our own.

Willingly leaving this matter to the decision of the public, since we cannot be umpires in our own cause, we proceed to detail such circumstances attending the writing and publication of our little work as may literally meet the wishes of the present proprietor of

PREFACE TO THE EIGHTEENTH EDITION

the copyright, who has applied to us for a gossiping Preface. Were we disposed to be grave and didactic, which is as foreign to our mood as it was twenty years ago, we might draw the attention of the reader, in a fine sententious paragraph, to the trifles upon which the fate of empires, as well as a four-and-sixpenny volume of parodies, occasionally hangs in trembling balance. No sooner was the idea of our work conceived, than it was about to be abandoned in embryo, from the apprehension that we had no time to mature and bring it forth, as it was indispensable that it should be written, printed, and published by the opening of Drury Lane Theatre, which would only allow us an interval of six weeks, and we had both of us other avocations that precluded us from the full command of even that limited period. Encouraged, however, by the conviction that the thought was a good one, and by the hope of making a lucky hit, we set to work *con amore*, our very hurry not improbably enabling us to strike out at a heat what we might have failed to produce so well, had we possessed time enough to hammer it into more careful and elaborate form.

Our first difficulty, that of selection, was by no means a light one. Some of our most eminent poets—such, for instance, as Rogers and Campbell—presented so much beauty, harmony, and proportion in their writings, both as to style and sentiment, that if we had attempted to caricature them, nobody would have recognised the likeness; and if we had endeavoured to give a servile copy of their manner, it would only have amounted, at best, to a tame and unamusing portrait, which it was not our object to present. Although fully aware that their names would, in the theatrical phrase, have conferred great strength upon our bill, we were reluctantly compelled to forgo them, and to confine ourselves to

PREFACE TO THE EIGHTEENTH EDITION

writers whose style and habit of thought, being more marked and peculiar, was more capable of exaggeration and distortion. To avoid politics and personality, to imitate the turn of mind as well as the phraseology of our originals, and, at all events, to raise a harmless laugh, were our main objects; in the attainment of which united aims we were sometimes hurried into extravagance, by attaching much more importance to the last than to the two first. In no instance were we thus betrayed into a greater injustice than in the case of Mr. Wordsworth—the touching sentiment, profound wisdom, and copious harmony of whose loftier writings we left unnoticed in the desire of burlesquing them; while we pounced upon his popular ballads, and exerted ourselves to push their simplicity into puerility and silliness. With pride and pleasure do we now claim to be ranked among the most ardent admirers of this true poet; and if he himself could see the state of his works, which are ever at our right hand, he would, perhaps, receive the manifest evidences they exhibit of constant reference and delighted re-perusal, as some sort of *amende honorable* for the unfairness of which we were guilty when we were less conversant with the higher inspirations of his muse. To Mr. Coleridge, and others of our originals, we must also do a tardy act of justice, by declaring that our burlesque of their peculiarities has never blinded us to those beauties and talents which are beyond the reach of all ridicule.

One of us[1] had written a genuine Address for the

---

[1] This was Horatio, the writer of the present Preface. The envelope which enclosed his Address to the Committee was sold with two volumes of the original Addresses at Mr. Winston's sale, Dec. 14, 1849, and was inscribed inside " Horatio Smith, 36, Basinghall Street."   P. C.

PREFACE TO THE EIGHTEENTH EDITION

occasion, which was sent to the Committee, and shared the fate it merited, in being rejected. To swell the bulk, or rather to diminish the tenuity of our little work, we added it to the Imitations; and prefixing the initials of S. T. P. for the purpose of puzzling the critics, were not a little amused, in the sequel, by the many guesses and conjectures into which we had ensnared some of our readers. We could even enjoy the mysticism, qualified as it was by the poor compliment, that our carefully written Address exhibited no " very prominent trait of absurdity," when we saw it thus noticed in the *Edinburgh Review* for November 1812:—"An Address by S. T. P. we can make nothing of; and professing our ignorance of the author designated by these letters, we can only add, that the Address, though a little affected, and not very full of meaning, has no very prominent trait of absurdity, that we can detect; and might have been adopted and spoken, so far as we can perceive, without any hazard of ridicule. In our simplicity we consider it as a very decent, mellifluous, occasional prologue; and do not understand how it has found its way into its present company."

Urged forward by hurry, and trusting to chance, two very bad coadjutors in any enterprise, we at length congratulated ourselves on having completed our task in time to have it printed and published by the opening of the theatre. But alas! our difficulties, so far from being surmounted, seemed only to be beginning. Strangers to the arcana of the booksellers' trade, and unacquainted with their almost invincible objection to single volumes of low price, especially when tendered by writers who have acquired no previous name, we little anticipated that they would refuse to publish our *Rejected Addresses*, even although we asked nothing for the copyright. Such,

PREFACE TO THE EIGHTEENTH EDITION

however, proved to be the case. Our manuscript was perused and returned to us by several of the most eminent publishers.[1] Well do we remember betaking ourselves to one of the craft in Bond-street, whom we found in a back parlour, with his gouty leg propped upon a cushion, in spite of which warning he diluted his luncheon with frequent glasses of Madeira. " What have you already written? " was his first question—an interrogatory to which we had been subjected in almost every instance. " Nothing by which we can be known." " Then I am afraid to undertake the publication." We presumed timidly to suggest that every writer must have a beginning, and that to refuse to publish for him until he had acquired a name was to imitate the sapient mother who cautioned her son against going into the water until he could swim. " An old joke—a regular Joe! " exclaimed our companion, tossing off another bumper. " Still older than Joe Miller," was our reply; " for, if we mistake not, it is the very first anecdote in the facetiæ of Hierocles." " Ha, sirs! " resumed the bibliopolist, " you are learned, are you? So, soh!—Well, leave your manuscript with me; I will look it over to-night, and give you an answer to-morrow." Punctual as

[1] The passage, as originally written, continued thus: " and among others, so difficult is it to form a correct judgment in catering to the public taste, by the very bibliopolist who has now, after an interval of twenty [*only* seven] years, purchased the copyright from a brother bookseller, and ventured upon the present edition." To this, on the proof-sheet, the late Mr. Murray appended the following note:—" I never saw or even had the MS. in my possession; but knowing that Mr. Smith was brother-in-law to Mr. Cadell, I took it for granted that the MS. had been previously offered to him and declined." Mr. H. Smith consequently drew his pen through the passage. P. C.

PREFACE TO THE EIGHTEENTH EDITION

the clock we presented ourselves at his door on the following morning, when our papers were returned to us with the observation—" These trifles are really not deficient in smartness; they are well, vastly well, for beginners; but they will never do—never. They would not pay for advertising, and without it I should not sell fifty copies."

This was discouraging enough. If the most experienced publishers feared to be out of pocket by the work, it was manifest, *à fortiori*, that its writers ran a risk of being still more heavy losers, should they undertake the publication on their own account. We had no objection to raise a laugh at the expense of others, but to do it at our own cost, uncertain as we were to what extent we might be involved, had never entered into our contemplation. In this dilemma, our *Addresses*, now in every sense rejected, might probably have never seen the light, had not some good angel whispered us to betake ourselves to Mr. John Miller, a dramatic publisher, then residing in Bow Street, Covent Garden. No sooner had this gentleman looked over our manuscript than he immediately offered to take upon himself all the risk of publication, and to give us half the profits, *should there be any;* a liberal proposition, with which we gladly closed. So rapid and decided was its success, at which none were more unfeignedly astonished than its authors, that Mr. Miller advised us to collect some *Imitations of Horace*, which had appeared anonymously in the *Monthly Mirror*,[1] offering to publish them upon the same terms. We did so accordingly; and as new editions of the *Rejected Addresses* were called for in

[1] Between 1807 and 1810. The *Monthly Mirror* was edited by Edward Du Bois, author of " My Pocket-Book," and by Thomas Hill; the original Paul Pry; and the Hull of Mr. Theodore Hook's novel of " Gilbert Gurney."   P. C.

PREFACE TO THE EIGHTEENTH EDITION

quick succession, we were shortly enabled to sell our half copyright in the two works to Mr. Miller for one thousand pounds!! We have entered into this unimportant detail, not to gratify any vanity of our own, but to encourage such literary beginners as may be placed in similar circumstances; as well as to impress upon publishers the propriety of giving more consideration to the possible merit of the works submitted to them, than to the mere magic of a name.

To the credit of the *genus irritabile* be it recorded, that not one of those whom we had parodied or burlesqued ever betrayed the least soreness on the occasion, or refused to join in the laugh that we had occasioned. With most of them we subsequently formed acquaintanceship; while some honoured us with an intimacy which still continues, where it has not been severed by the rude hand of Death. Alas! it is painful to reflect, that of the twelve writers whom we presumed to imitate, five are now no more; the list of the deceased being unhappily swelled by the most illustrious of all, the *clarum et venerabile nomen* of Sir Walter Scott! From that distinguished writer, whose transcendent talents were only to be equalled by his virtues and his amiability, we received favours and notice, both public and private, which it will be difficult to forget, because we had not the smallest claim upon his kindness. " I certainly must have written this myself! " said that fine-tempered man to one of the authors, pointing to the description of the Fire, " although I forget upon what occasion." Lydia White,[1] a literary

---

[1] Miss Lydia White, celebrated for her lively wit and for her blue-stocking parties, unrivalled, it is said, in " the soft realm of *blue* May Fair." She died in 1827, and is mentioned in the diaries of Scott and Byron. P. C.

PREFACE TO THE EIGHTEENTH EDITION

lady who was prone to feed the lions of the day, invited one of us to dinner; but, recollecting afterwards that William Spencer[1] formed one of the party, wrote to the latter to put him off, telling him that a man was to be at her table whom he " would not like to meet." " Pray, who is this whom I should not like to meet? " inquired the poet. " O! " answered the lady, " one of those men who have made that shameful attack upon you! " " The very man upon earth I should like to know! " rejoined the lively and careless bard. The two individuals accordingly met, and have continued fast friends ever since. Lord Byron, too, wrote thus to Mr. Murray from Italy—" Tell him I forgive him, were he twenty times over our satirist."

It may not be amiss to notice, in this place, one criticism of a Leicestershire clergyman, which may be pronounced unique: " I do not see why they should have been rejected," observed the matter-of-fact annotator; " I think some of them very good! " Upon the whole, few have been the instances, in the acrimonious history of literature, where a malicious pleasantry like the *Rejected Addresses*—which the parties ridiculed might well consider more annoying than a direct satire—instead of being met by querulous bitterness or petulant retaliation, has procured for its authors the acquaintance, or conciliated the good-will, of those whom they had the most audaciously burlesqued.

In commenting on a work, however trifling, which has survived the lapse of twenty years, an author may almost claim the privileged garrulity of age; yet even in a professedly gossiping Preface, we begin to fear that we are exceeding our commission, and abusing the patience of the reader. If we are doing so, we might

[1] See note on " The Beautiful Incendiary," p. 156.

PREFACE TO THE EIGHTEENTH EDITION

urge extenuating circumstances, which will explain, though they may not excuse, our diffuseness. To one of us the totally unexpected success of this little work proved an important event, since it mainly decided him, some years afterwards, to embark in the literary career which the continued favour of that novel-reading world has rendered both pleasant and profitable to him. This is the first, as it will probably be the last, occasion upon which we shall ever intrude ourselves personally on the public notice; and we trust that our now doing so will stand excused by the reasons we have adduced. For the portraits prefixed to this edition we are in no way responsible. At the sale of the late Mr. Marlowe's effects, the drawing from which they are engraved was purchased by Mr. Murray who, conceiving probably that we had no interest in the matter—since they were not likenesses of our present heads but of those which we possessed twenty years ago—has thought proper to give them publicity, without consulting their now rather antiquated originals.

LONDON, *March*, 1833   [HORACE SMITH]

This book was originally published in Oct. 1812.

ADVERTISEMENT TO THE TWENTY-SECOND EDITION

James Smith and Horace Smith, authors of the *Rejected Addresses; or, The New Theatrum Poetarum*, were the sons of Robert Smith, solicitor to the Board of Ordnance. James was born at No. 36, Basinghall Street, London, on the 10th of February, 1775; and Horace in the same house on the 31st of December, 1779.

James was educated under the Rev. Mr. Burford at Chigwell in Essex; articled to his father on leaving school, subsequently taken into partnership with him, and eventually succeeded to his father's business, as well as his appointment of solicitor to the Ordnance. Horace received the same education as his brother, became a member of the Stock Exchange in London, acquired a fortune, and retired with his wife and family to Brighton. James, who lived and died single, was the author of several small copies of verses, since collected by his brother; and Horace was the author of " Brambletye House," a novel in three volumes, well received at the time of its publication.

The work by which the brothers are best known, and by which they will continue to be remembered, is the *Rejected Addresses*. This delightful volume—one of the luckiest hits in literature—appeared on the re-opening of Drury Lane Theatre, in October, 1812; the idea, as Horace relates, having been casually started by the late Mr. Ward, secretary to the theatre, exactly six weeks before the night when the opening Address was to be

ADVERTISEMENT TO 22ND EDITION

spoken. The hint thus thrown out was eagerly adopted. The brothers arranged what authors they should respectively imitate; and James executed his portion in London, and Horace the remainder at Cheltenham. James supplied the imitations of Wordsworth, Southey, Coleridge, Crabbe, and Cobbett, and Nos. 14, 16, 18, 19, and 20. The Byron was a joint effusion—James contributing the first stanza, and Horace the remainder. The Fitzgerald, the Sir Walter Scott, &c., were by Horace. The corrections which each supplied to the compositions of the other seldom exceeded verbal alterations or the addition of a few lines.

The copyright, which had been originally offered to Mr. Murray for 20*l.*, and refused without even looking at the MS., was purchased by that gentleman in 1819, after the book had run through sixteen editions, for 131*l.*

James Smith died at his house, No. 27, Craven Street, Strand, on the 24th December, 1839, in the 65th year of his age; and was buried in the vaults of the church of St. Martin's in the Fields. Horace died at Tunbridge Wells, on the 12th of July, 1849, in the 70th year of his age, and was buried in the churchyard of Trinity Church, Tunbridge Wells.

P. C.
[PETER CUNNINGHAM]

CONTENTS

		PAGE
I.	Loyal Effusion. By W. T. F.	37
II.	The Baby's Debut. By W. W.	40
III.	An Address without a Phœnix. By S. T. P.	44
IV.	Cui Bono? By Lord B.	46
V.	Hampshire Farmer's Address. By W. C.	51
VI.	The Living Lustres. By T. M.	56
VII.	The Rebuilding. By R. S.	59
VIII.	Drury's Dirge. By L. M.	66
IX.	A Tale of Drury Lane. By W. S.	70
X.	Johnson's Ghost	78
XI.	The Beautiful Incendiary. By the Hon. W. S.	83
XII.	Fire and Ale. By M. G. L.	87
XIII.	Playhouse Musings. By S. T. C.	90
XIV.	Drury's Hustings	94
XV.	Architectural Atoms. By Dr. B.	97
XVI.	Theatrical Alarm Bell. By M. P.	105
XVII.	The Theatre. By the Rev. G. C.	109
XVIII.	Macbeth Travestie. By M. M.	116
XIX.	Stranger Travestie. By Ditto	120
XX.	George Barnwell Travestie. By Ditto	122
XXI.	Punch's Apotheosis. By T. H.	125

REJECTED ADDRESSES

William Thomas Fitz Gerald Esqr

LOYAL EFFUSION
BY W. T. F.

" Quicquid dicunt, laudo: id rursum si negant.
Laudo id quoque."   TERENCE.

H A I L , glorious edifice, stupendous work!
God bless the Regent and the Duke of York!
  Ye Muses! by whose aid I cried down Fox,
Grant me in Drury Lane a private box,
Where I may loll, cry bravo! and profess
The boundless powers of England's glorious press;
While Afric's sons exclaim, from shore to shore,
" Quashee ma boo! "—the slave-trade is no more!
  In fair Arabia (happy once, now stony),
Since ruined by that arch apostate Boney),
A phœnix late was caught: the Arab host
Long ponder'd—part would boil it, part would roast;
But while they ponder, up the pot-lid flies,
Fledged, beak'd, and claw'd, alive they see him rise
To heaven, and caw defiance in the skies.
So Drury, first in roasting flames consumed,
Then by old renters to hot water doom'd,
By Wyatt's trowel patted, plump and sleek,
Soars without wings, and caws without a beak.
Gallia's stern despot shall in vain advance
From Paris, the metropolis of France;
By this day month the monster shall not gain
A foot of land in Portugal or Spain.
See Wellington in Salamanca's field
Forces his favourite general to yield,

Breaks through his lines, and leaves his boasted Marmont
Expiring on the plain without his arm on;
Madrid he enters at the cannon's mouth,
And then the villages still further south.
Base Buonapartè, fill'd with deadly ire,
Sets, one by one, our playhouses on fire.
Some years ago he pounced with deadly glee on
The Opera House, then burnt down the Pantheon;
Nay, still unsated, in a coat of flames,
Next at Milbank he cross'd the river Thames;
Thy hatch, O Halfpenny! pass'd in a trice,
Boil'd some black pitch, and burnt down Astley's twice;
Then buzzing on through ether with a vile hum,
Turn'd to the left hand, fronting the Asylum,
And burnt the Royal Circus in a hurry—
('Twas call'd the Circus then, but now the Surrey).

   Who burnt (confound his soul!) the houses twain
Of Covent Garden and of Drury Lane?
Who, while the British squadron lay off Cork
(God bless the Regent and the Duke of York!)
With a foul earthquake ravaged the Caraccas,
And raised the price of dry goods and tobaccos?
Who makes the quartern loaf and Luddites rise?
Who fills the butchers' shops with large blue flies?
Who thought in flames St. James's court to pinch?
Who burnt the wardrobe of poor Lady Finch?—
Why he, who, forging for this isle a yoke,
Reminds me of a line I lately spoke,
" The tree of freedom is the British oak."

   Bless every man possess'd of aught to give;
Long may Long Tilney Wellesley Long Pole live;
God bless the Army, bless their coats of scarlet,
God bless the Navy, bless the Princess Charlotte;

LOYAL EFFUSION

God bless the Guards, though worsted Gallia scoff,
God bless their pig-tails, though they're now cut off;
And, oh! in Downing Street should Old Nick revel,
England's prime minister, then bless the devil!

THE BABY'S DEBUT
BY W. W.

" Thy lisping prattle and thy mincing gait,
All thy false mimic fooleries I hate;
For thou art Folly's counterfeit, and she
Who is right foolish hath the better plea:
Nature's true idiot I prefer to thee."
                                        CUMBERLAND.

*[Spoken in the character of Nancy Lake, a girl eight years
of age, who is drawn upon the stage in a child's chaise
by Samuel Hughes, her uncle's porter.]*

    M Y brother Jack was nine in May,
    And I was eight on New-year's-day;
       So in Kate Wilson's shop
    Papa (he's my papa and Jack's)
    Bought me, last week, a doll of wax,
       And brother Jack a top.

    Jack's in the pouts, and this it is,—
    He thinks mine came to more than his;
       So to my drawer he goes,
    Takes out the doll, and, O, my stars!
    He pokes her head between the bars,
       And melts off half her nose!

    Quite cross, a bit of string I beg,
    And tie it to his peg-top's peg,
       And bang, with might and main,

Wm Wordsworth

THE BABY'S DEBUT

Its head against the parlour-door:
Off flies the head, and hits the floor,
    And breaks a window-pane.

This made him cry with rage and spite:
Well, let him cry, it serves him right.
    A pretty thing, forsooth!
If he's to melt, all scalding hot,
Half my doll's nose, and I am not
    To draw his peg-top's tooth!

Aunt Hannah heard the window break,
And cried, " O naughty Nancy Lake,
    Thus to distress your aunt:
No Drury-Lane for you to-day!"
And while papa said, " Pooh, she may!"
    Mamma said, " No, she sha'n't!"

Well, after many a sad reproach,
They got into a hackney coach,
    And trotted down the street.
I saw them go: one horse was blind,
The tails of both hung down behind,
    Their shoes were on their feet.

The chaise in which poor brother Bill
Used to be drawn to Pentonville,
    Stood in the lumber-room:
I wiped the dust from off the top,
While Molly mopp'd it with a mop,
    And brush'd it with a broom.

My uncle's porter, Samuel Hughes,
Came in at six to black the shoes,
    (I always talk to Sam:)

So what does he, but takes, and drags
Me in the chaise along the flags,
    And leaves me where I am.

My father's walls are made of brick,
But not so tall and not so thick
    As these; and, goodness me!
My father's beams are made of wood,
But never, never half so good
    As those that now I see.

What a large floor! 'tis like a town!
The carpet when they lay it down,
    Won't hide it, I'll be bound;
And there's a row of lamps!—my eye!
How they do blaze! I wonder why
    They keep them on the ground.

At first I caught hold of the wing,
And kept away; but Mr. Thing-
    umbob, the prompter man,
Gave with his hand my chaise a shove,
And said, " Go on, my pretty love;
    " Speak to' em, little Nan.

" You've only got to curtsy, whisp-
er, hold your chin up, laugh, and lisp,
    And then you're sure to take:
I've known the day when brats, not quite
Thirteen, got fifty pounds a-night;
    Then why not Nancy Lake? "

But while I'm speaking, where's papa?
And where's my aunt? and where's mamma?
    Where's Jack? O, there they sit!

THE BABY'S DEBUT

They smile, they nod; I'll go my ways,
And order round poor Billy's chaise,
    To join them in the pit.

And now, good gentlefolks, I go
To join mamma, and see the show;
    So, bidding you adieu,
I curtsy, like a pretty miss,
And if you'll blow to me a kiss,
    I'll blow a kiss to you.
          [*Blows a kiss, and exit.*]

AN ADDRESS WITHOUT A PHŒNIX
BY S. T. P.

" This was looked for at your hand, and this was balked." *What you Will.*

W H A T stately vision mocks my waking sense?
Hence, dear delusion, sweet enchantment, hence!
Ha! is it real?—can my doubts be vain?
It is, it is, and Drury lives again!
Around each grateful veteran attends,
Eager to rush and gratulate his friends,
Friends whose kind looks, retraced with proud delight,
Endear the past, and make the future bright:
Yes, generous patrons, your returning smile
Blesses our toils, and consecrates our pile.

When last we met, Fate's unrelenting hand
Already grasped the devastating brand;
Slow crept the silent flame, ensnared its prize,
Then burst resistless to the astonished skies.
The glowing walls, disrobed of scenic pride,
In trembling conflict stemmed the burning tide,
Till crackling, blazing, rocking to its fall,
Down rushed the thundering roof, and buried all!

Where late the sister Muses sweetly sung,
And raptured thousands on their music hung,
Where Wit and Wisdom shone, by Beauty graced,
Sat lonely Silence, empress of the waste;

AN ADDRESS WITHOUT A PHŒNIX

And still had reigned—but he, whose voice can raise
More magic wonders than Amphion's lays,
Bade jarring bands with friendly zeal engage
To rear the prostrate glories of the stage.
Up leaped the Muses at the potent spell,
And Drury's genius saw his temple swell;
Worthy, we hope, the British Drama's cause,
Worthy of British arts, and *your* applause.

   Guided by you, our earnest aims presume
To renovate the Drama with the dome;
The scenes of Shakespeare and our bards of old,
With due observance splendidly unfold,
Yet raise and foster with parental hand
The living talent of our native land.
O! may we still, to sense and nature true,
Delight the many, nor offend the few.
Though varying tastes our changeful Drama claim,
Still be its moral tendency the same,
To win by precept, by example warn,
To brand the front of Vice with pointed scorn,
And Virtue's smiling brows with votive wreaths adorn.

CUI BONO?

BY LORD B.

I

S A T E D with home, of wife, of children tired,
The restless soul is driven abroad to roam;
Sated abroad, all seen, yet nought admired,
The restless soul is driven to ramble home;
Sated with both, beneath new Drury's dome
The fiend Ennui awhile consents to pine,
There growls, and curses, like a deadly Gnome,
Scorning to view fantastic Columbine,
Viewing with scorn and hate the nonsense of the Nine.

II

Ye reckless dupes, who hither wend your way
To gaze on puppets in a painted dome,

CUI BONO?

Pursuing pastimes glittering to betray,
Like falling stars in life's eternal gloom,
What seek ye here? Joy's evanescent bloom?
Woe's me! the brightest wreaths she ever gave
Are but as flowers that decorate a tomb.
Man's heart, the mournful urn o'er which they wave,
Is sacred to despair, its pedestal the grave.

III

Has life so little store of real woes,
That here ye wend to taste fictitious grief?
Or is it that from truth such anguish flows,
Ye court the lying drama for relief?
Long shall ye find the pang, the respite brief:
Or if one tolerable page appears
In folly's volume, 'tis the actor's leaf,
Who dries his own by drawing others' tears,
And, raising present mirth, makes glad his future years.

IV

Albeit, how like young Betty doth he flee!
Light as the mote that daunceth in the beam,
He liveth only in man's present e'e,
His life a flash, his memory a dream,
Oblivious down he drops in Lethe's stream.
Yet what are they, the learned and the great?
Awhile of longer wonderment the theme!
Who shall presume to prophesy *their* date,
Where nought is certain, save the uncertainty of fate?

V

This goodly pile, upheaved by Wyatt's toil,
Perchance than Holland's edifice more fleet,

Again red Lemnos' artisan may spoil;
The fire-alarm and midnight drum may beat,
And all be strewed ysmoking at your feet!
Start ye? perchance Death's angel may be sent,
Ere from the flaming temple ye retreat;
And ye who met, on revel idlesse bent,
May find, in pleasure's fane, your grave and monument.

VI

Your debts mount high—ye plunge in deeper waste;
The tradesman duns—no warning voice ye hear;
The plaintiff sues—to public shows ye haste;
The bailiff threats—ye feel no idle fear.
Who can arrest your prodigal career?
Who can keep down the levity of youth?
What sound can startle age's stubborn ear?
Who can redeem from wretchedness and ruth
Men true to falsehood's voice, false to the voice of truth?

VII

To thee, blest saint! who doffed thy skin to make
The Smithfield rabble leap from theirs with joy,
We dedicate the pile—arise! awake!—
Knock down the Muses, wit and sense destroy,
Clear our new stage from reason's dull alloy,
Charm hobbling age, and tickle capering youth
With cleaver, marrow-bone, and Tunbridge toy;
While, vibrating in unbelieving tooth,
Harps' twang in Drury's walls, and make her boards a booth.

VIII

For what is Hamlet, but a hare in March?
And what is Brutus, but a croaking owl?

Lord Byron

CUI BONO?

And what is Rolla? Cupid steeped in starch,
Orlando's helmet in Augustin's cowl.
Shakespeare, how true thine adage, " fair is foul! "
To him whose soul is with fruition fraught,
The song of Braham is an Irish howl,
Thinking is but an idle waste of thought,
And nought is every thing, and every thing is nought.

IX

Sons of Parnassus! whom I view above,
Not laurel-crown'd, but clad in rusty black;
Not spurring Pegasus through Tempè's grove,
But pacing Grub-street on a jaded hack;
What reams of foolscap, while your brains ye rack,
Ye mar to make again! for sure, ere long,
Condemn'd to tread the bard's time-sanction'd track,
Ye all shall join the bailiff-haunted throng,
And reproduce, in rags, the rags ye blot in song.

X

So fares the follower in the Muses' train;
He toils to starve, and only lives in death;
We slight him, till our patronage is vain,
Then round his skeleton a garland wreathe,
And o'er his bones an empty requiem breathe—
Oh! with what tragic horror would he start,
(Could he be conjured from the grave beneath)
To find the stage again a Thespian cart,
And elephants and colts down trampling Shakespeare's art.

XI

Hence, pedant Nature! with thy Grecian rules!
Centaurs (not fabulous) those rules efface;

CUI BONO?

Back, sister Muses, to your native schools;
Here booted grooms usurp Apollo's place,
Hoofs shame the boards that Garrick used to grace,
The play of limbs succeeds the play of wit,
Man yields the drama to the Hou'yn'm race,
His prompter spurs, his licenser the bit,
The stage a stable-yard, a jockey-club the pit.

XII

Is it for these ye rear this proud abode?
Is it for these your superstition seeks
To build a temple worthy of a god,
To laud a monkey, or to worship leeks?
Then be the stage, to recompense your freaks,
A motley chaos, jumbling age and ranks,
Where Punch, the lignum-vitæ Roscius, squeaks,
And Wisdom weeps, and Folly plays her pranks,
And moody Madness laughs and hugs the chain he clanks.

TO THE SECRETARY
OF THE MANAGING COMMITTEE OF
DRURY-LANE PLAYHOUSE

SIR,
    To the gewgaw fetters of *rhyme* (invented by the monks to enslave the people) I have a rooted objection. I have therefore written an address for your theatre in plain, homespun, yeoman's *prose;* in the doing whereof I hope I am swayed by nothing but an *independent* wish to open the eyes of this gulled people, to prevent a repetition of the dramatic *bamboozling* they have hitherto laboured under. If you like what I have done, and mean to make use of it, I don't want any such *aristocratic* reward as a piece of plate with two griffins sprawling upon it, or a *dog* and a *jackass* fighting for a ha'p'worth of *gilt gingerbread*, or any such Bartholomew-fair nonsense. All I ask is, that the door-keepers of your playhouse may take all the *sets of my Register* now on hand, and *force* every body who enters your doors to buy one, giving afterwards a debtor and creditor account of what they have received, *post-paid*, and in due course remitting me the money and unsold Registers, *carriage-paid*.

                              I am, &c.
                                  W. C.

IN THE CHARACTER OF
A HAMPSHIRE FARMER

———— " Rabidâ qui concitus irâ
Implevit pariter ternis latratibus auras,
Et sparsit virides spumis albentibus agros."
OVID.

MOST THINKING PEOPLE,
WHEN persons address an audience from the stage, it is usual, either in words or gesture, to say, " Ladies and Gentlemen, your servant." If I were base enough, mean enough, paltry enough, and *brute beast* enough, to follow that fashion, I should tell two lies in a breath. In the first place, you are *not* Ladies and Gentlemen, but I hope something better, that is to say, honest men and women; and in the next place, if you were ever so much ladies, and ever so much gentlemen, I am not, *nor ever will be*, your humble servant. You see me here, *most thinking people*, by mere chance. I have not been within the doors of a playhouse before for these ten years; nor, till that abominable custom of taking money at the doors is discontinued, will I ever sanction a theatre with my presence. The stage-door is the only gate of *freedom* in the whole edifice, and through that I made my way from Bagshaw's in Brydges Street, to accost you. Look about you. Are you not all comfortable? Nay, never slink, mun; speak out, if you are dissatisfied, and tell me so before I leave town. You are now, (thanks to *Mr. Whitbread*), got into a large, comfortable house. Not into a *gimcrack palace;* not into a *Solomon's temple;*

William Cobbett Esqr

not into a frost-work of Brobdignag filigree; but into a plain, honest, homely, industrious, wholesome, *brown brick playhouse.* You have been struggling for independence and elbow-room these three years; and who gave it you? Who helped you out of Lilliput? Who routed you from a rat-hole, five inches by four, to perch you in a palace? Again and again I answer, *Mr. Whitbread.* You might have sweltered in that place with the Greek name till doomsday, and neither *Lord Castlereagh*, *Mr. Canning*, no, nor the *Marquess Wellesley*, would have turned a trowel to help you out! Remember that. Never forget that. Read it to your children, and to your children's children! And now, *most thinking people*, cast your eyes over my head to what the builder, (I beg his pardon, the architect), calls the *proscenium*. No motto, no slang, no popish Latin, to keep the people in the dark. No *veluti in speculum.* Nothing in the dead languages, properly so called, for they ought to die, ay and be *damned* to boot! The Covent Garden manager tried that, and a pretty business he made of it! When a man says *veluti in speculum*, he is called a man of letters. Very well, and is not a man who cries O. P. a man of letters too? You ran your O. P. against his *veluti in speculum*, and pray which beat? I prophesied that, though I never told any body. I take it for granted, that every intelligent man, woman, and child, to whom I address myself, has stood severally and respectively in Little Russell Street, and cast their, his, her, and its eyes on the outside of this building before they paid their money to view the inside. Look at the brickwork, *English Audience!* Look at the brickwork! All plain and smooth like a quakers' meeting. None of your Egyptian pyramids, to entomb subscribers' capitals. No overgrown colonnades of stone, like an alderman's gouty legs in white cotton stockings, fit only to use as rammers for paving Tottenham Court Road. This house is neither after the model of a temple in Athens, no, nor a *temple* in *Moorfields*, but it is built to act English plays in; and, provided you have good scenery, dresses, and decorations, I daresay you wouldn't break your hearts if the outside were as plain as the pikestaff I used to carry when I was a sergeant. *Apropos*, as the French valets say, who cut their masters' throats—*apropos*, a word about dresses. You must, many of you, have seen what I have read a description of, Kemble and Mrs. Siddons in Macbeth, with more gold and silver plastered on their doublets than would have kept an honest family in butcher's meat and flannel from year's end to year's end! I am informed, (now mind, I do not vouch for the fact), but I am informed that all such extravagant idleness is to be done away with here. Lady Macbeth is to have a plain quilted petticoat, a cotton gown, and a *mob cap* (as the court parasites call it;—it will be well for them, if, one of these days, they don't wear a mob cap—I mean a *white cap*, with a *mob* to look at them); and Macbeth is to appear in an honest yeoman's drab coat, and a pair of black calamanco breeches. Not *Sal*amanca; no, nor *Talavera* neither, my most Noble Marquess; but plain, honest, black calamanco stuff breeches. This is right; this is as it should be. *Most thinking people*, I have heard you much abused. There is not a compound in the language but is strung fifty in a rope, like onions, by the Morning Post, and hurled in your teeth. You are called the mob; and when they have made you out to be the mob, you are called the *scum* of the people, and the *dregs* of the people. I should like to know how you can be both. Take a basin of broth— not *cheap soup*, Mr. *Wilberforce*—not soup for the poor,

HAMPSHIRE FARMER'S ADDRESS

at a penny a quart, as your mixture of horses' legs, brick-dust, and old shoes, was denominated—but plain, wholesome, patriotic beef or mutton broth; take this, examine it, and you will find—mind, I don't vouch for the fact, but I am told—you will find the dregs at the bottom, and the scum at the top. I will endeavour to explain this to you: England is a large *earthenware pipkin;* John Bull is the *beef* thrown into it; taxes are the *hot water* he boils in; rotten boroughs are the *fuel* that blazes under this same pipkin; parliament is the *ladle* that stirs the hodge-podge, and sometimes———. But, hold! I don't wish to pay *Mr. Newman* a second visit. I leave you better off than you have been this many a day: you have a good house over your head; you have beat the French in Spain; the harvest has turned out well; the comet keeps its distance; and red slippers are hawked about in Constantinople for next to nothing; and for all this, *again and again* I tell you, you are indebted to *Mr. Whitbread!!!*

THE LIVING LUSTRES
BY T. M.

" Jam te juvaverit
 Viros relinquere,
 Doctæque conjugis
 Sinu quiescere."
                    Sir T. More.

I
O W H Y should our dull retrospective addresses
  Fall damp as wet blankets on Drury Lane fire?
Away with blue devils, away with distresses,
  And give the gay spirit to sparkling desire!

II
Let artists decide on the beauties of Drury,
  The richest to me is when woman is there;
The question of houses I leave to the jury;
  The fairest to me is the house of the fair.

III
When woman's soft smile all our senses bewilders,
  And gilds, while it carves, her dear form on the heart,
What need has New Drury of carvers and gilders?
  With Nature so bounteous, why call upon Art?

IV
How well would our actors attend to their duties,
  Our house save in oil, and our authors in wit,
In lieu of yon lamps, if a row of young beauties
  Glanced light from their eyes between us and the pit!

T Moore

THE LIVING LUSTRES

V

The apples that grew on the fruit-tree of knowledge
   By woman were pluck'd, and she still wears the prize,
To tempt us in theatre, senate, or college—
   I mean the love-apples that bloom in the eyes.

VI

There too is the lash which, all statutes controlling,
   Still governs the slaves that are made by the fair;
For man is the pupil, who, while her eye's rolling,
   Is lifted to rapture, or sunk in despair.

VII

Bloom, Theatre, bloom, in the roseate blushes
   Of beauty illumed by a love-breathing smile;
And flourish, ye pillars, as green as the rushes
   That pillow the nymphs of the Emerald Isle!

VIII

For dear is the Emerald Isle of the ocean,
   Whose daughters are fair as the foam of the wave,
Whose sons, unaccustom'd to rebel commotion,
   Though joyous, are sober—though peaceful are brave.

IX

The shamrock their olive, sworn foe to a quarrel,
   Protects from the thunder and lightning of rows;
Their sprig of shillelagh is nothing but laurel,
   Which flourishes rapidly over their brows.

X

O! soon shall they burst the tyrannical shackles
   Which each panting bosom indignantly names,
Until not one goose at the capital cackles
   Against the grand question of Catholic claims.

REJECTED ADDRESSES

XI

And then shall each Paddy, who once on the Liffy
    Perchance held the helm of some mackerel-hoy,
Hold the helm of the state, and dispense in a jiffy
    More fishes than ever he caught when a boy.

XII

And those who now quit their hods, shovels, and bar-
    rows,
    In crowds to the bar of some ale-house to flock,
When bred to *our* bar shall be Gibbses and Garrows,
    Assume the silk gown, and discard the smock-frock.

XIII

For Erin surpasses the daughters of Neptune,
    As Dian outshines each encircling star;
And the spheres of the heavens could never have kept
    tune
    Till set to the music of Erin-go-bragh!

THE REBUILDING
BY R. S.

——— " Per audaces nova dithyrambos
Verba devolvit, numerisque fertur
Lege solutis."   HORAT.

[Spoken by a Glendoveer.]

I AM a blessed Glendoveer:
'Tis mine to speak, and yours to hear.
    Midnight, yet not a nose
From Tower-hill to Piccadilly snored!
    Midnight, yet not a nose
From Indra drew the essence of repose!
    See with what crimson fury,
By Indra fann'd, the god of fire ascends the walls of
                Drury!

    Tops of houses, blue with lead,
    Bend beneath the landlord's tread.
Master and 'prentice, serving-man and lord,
      Nailor and tailor,
      Grazier and brazier,
    Through streets and alleys pour'd—
      All, all abroad to gaze,
      And wonder at the blaze.
    Thick calf, fat foot, and slim knee,
    Mounted on roof and chimney,
    The mighty roast, the mighty stew
        To see;

As if the dismal view
Were but to them a Brentford jubilee.

Vainly, all-radiant Surya, sire of Phaeton
(By Greeks call'd Apollo)
Hollow
Sounds from thy harp proceed;
Combustible as reed,
The tongue of Vulcan licks thy wooden legs:
From Drury's top, dissever'd from thy pegs,
Thou tumblest,
Humblest,
Where late thy bright effulgence shone on high;
While, by thy somerset excited, fly
Ten million
Billion
Sparks from the pit, to gem the sable sky.

Now come the men of fire to quench the fires:
To Russell Street see Globe and Atlas run,
Hope gallops first, and second Sun;
On flying heel,
See Hand-in-Hand
O'ertake the band!
View with what glowing wheel
He nicks
Phœnix!

While Albion scampers from Bridge Street, Blackfriars—
Drury Lane! Drury Lane!
Drury Lane! Drury Lane!
They shout and they bellow again and again.
All, all in vain!
Water turns steam;
Each blazing beam

Robert Southey

THE REBUILDING

Hisses defiance to the eddying spout:
It seems but too plain that nothing can put it out!
Drury Lane! Drury Lane!
See, Drury Lane expires!

Pent in by smoke-dried beams, twelve moons or more,
Shorn of his ray,
Surya in durance lay:
The workmen heard him shout,
But thought it would not pay,
To dig him out.
When lo! terrific Yamen, lord of hell,
Solemn as lead,
Judge of the dead,
Sworn foe to witticism,
By men call'd criticism,
Came passing by that way:
Rise! cried the fiend, behold a sight of gladness!
Behold the rival theatre!
I've set O. P. at her,
Who, like a bull-dog bold,
Growls and fastens on his hold.
The many-headed rabble roar in madness;
Thy rival staggers: come and spy her
Deep in the mud as thou art in the mire.
So saying, in his arms he caught the beaming one,
And crossing Russell Street,
He placed him on his feet
'Neath Covent Garden dome. Sudden a sound,
As of the bricklayers of Babel, rose:
Horns, rattles, drums, tin trumpets, sheets of copper,
Punches and slaps, thwacks of all sorts and sizes,
From the knobb'd bludgeon to the taper switch,
Ran echoing round the walls; paper placards

Blotted the lamps, boots brown with mud the benches;
A sea of heads roll'd roaring in the pit;
On paper wings O. P.'s
Reclin'd in lettered ease;
While shout and scoff,
Ya! ya! off! off!
Like thunderbolt on Surya's ear-drum fell,
And seem'd to paint
The savage oddities of Saint
Bartholomew in hell.

Tears dimm'd the god of light—
" Bear me back, Yamen, from this hideous sight;
Bear me back, Yamen, I grow sick,
Oh! bury me again in brick;
Shall I on New Drury tremble,
To be O. P.'d like Kemble?
No,
Better remain by rubbish guarded,
Than thus hubbubish groan placarded;
Bear me back, Yamen, bear me quick,
And bury me again in brick."
Obedient Yamen
Answered, " Amen,"
And did
As he was bid.

There lay the buried god, and Time
Seemed to decree eternity of lime;
But pity, like a dew-drop, gently prest
Almighty Veeshnoo's adamantine breast:
He, the preserver, ardent still
To do whate'er he says he will,
From South-hill wing'd his way,
To raise the drooping lord of day.

THE REBUILDING

All earthly spells the busy one o'erpower'd;
He treats with men of all conditions,
Poets and players, tradesmen, and musicians;
Nay, even ventures
To attack the renters,
Old and new;
A list he gets
Of claims and debts,
And deems nought done, while aught remains to do.
Yamen beheld, and wither'd at the sight;
Long had he aim'd the sunbeam to control,
For light was hateful to his soul:
" Go on! " cried the hellish one, yellow with spite;
" Go on! " cried the hellish one, yellow with spleen,
" Thy toils of the morning, like Ithaca's queen,
I'll toil to undo every night."

Ye sons of song, rejoice!
Veeshnoo has still'd the jarring elements,
The spheres hymn music;
Again the god of day
Peeps forth with trembling ray,
Wakes, from their humid caves, the sleeping Nine,
And pours at intervals a strain divine.
" I have an iron yet in the fire," cried Yamen;
" The vollied flame rides in my breath,
My blast is elemental death;
This hand shall tear your paper bonds to pieces;
Ingross your deeds, assignments, leases,
My breath shall every line erase
Soon as I blow the blaze."
The lawyers are met at the Crown and Anchor,
And Yamen's visage grows blanker and blanker
The lawyers are met at the Anchor and Crown,

And Yamen's cheek is a russety brown:
Veshnoo, now thy work proceeds;
The solicitor reads,
And, merit of merit!
Red wax and green ferret
Are fixed at the foot of the deeds!
Yamen beheld and shiver'd;
His finger and thumb were cramped;
His ear by the flea in't was bitten,
When he saw by the lawyer's clerk written,
Sealed and delivered,
Being first duly stamped.
" Now for my turn! " the demon cries, and blows
A blast of sulphur from his mouth and nose.
Ah! bootless aim! the critic fiend,
Sagacious Yamen, judge of hell,
Is judged in his turn;
Parchment won't burn!
His schemes of vengeance are dissolv'd in air,
Parchment won't tear!!

Is it not written in the Himakoot book,
(That mighty Baly from Kehama took)
" Who blows on pounce
Must the Swerga renounce? "
It is! it is! Yamen, thine hour is nigh:
Like as an eagle claws an asp,
Veeshnoo has caught him in his mighty grasp,
And hurl'd him, in spite of his shrieks and his squalls,
Whizzing aloft, like the Temple fountain,
Three times as high as Meru mountain,
Which is
Ninety-nine times as high as St. Paul's.
Descending, he twisted like Levy the Jew,

THE REBUILDING

Who a durable grave meant
To dig in the pavement
Of Monument-yard:
To earth by the laws of attraction he flew,
And he fell, and he fell
To the regions of hell;
Nine centuries bounced he from cavern to rock,
And his head, as he tumbled, went nickety-nock,
Like a pebble in Carisbrook well.

Now Veeshnoo turn'd round to a capering varlet,
Arrayed in blue and white and scarlet,
And cried, " Oh! brown of slipper as of hat!
Lend me, Harlequin, thy bat! "
He seized the wooden sword, and smote the earth;
When lo! upstarting into birth
A fabric, gorgeous to behold,
Outshone in elegance the old,
And Veeshnoo saw, and cried, "Hail, playhouse mine!"
Then, bending his head, to Surya he said:
" Soon as thy maiden sister Di
Caps with her copper lid the dark blue sky,
And through the fissures of her clouded fan
Peeps at the naughty monster man,
Go mount yon edifice,
And shew thy steady face
In renovated pride,
More bright, more glorious than before!"
But ah! coy Surya still felt a twinge,
Still smarted from his former singe;
And to Veeshnoo replied,
In a tone rather gruff,
' No, thank you! one tumble's enough!"

DRURY'S DIRGE

BY LAURA MATILDA

"You praise our sires: but though they wrote with force,
Their rhymes were vicious, and their diction coarse:
We want their *strength*, agreed; but we atone
For that and more, by *sweetness* all our own."
GIFFORD.

I

BALMY Zephyrs, lightly flitting,
Shade me with your azure wing;

Mrs COWLEY

DRURY'S DIRGE

On Parnassus' summit sitting,
  Aid me, Clio, while I sing.

II

Softly slept the dome of Drury
  O'er the empyreal crest,
When Alecto's sister-fury
  Softly slumb'ring sunk to rest.

III

Lo! from Lemnos limping lamely,
  Lags the lowly Lord of Fire,
Cytherea yielding tamely
  To the Cyclops dark and dire.

IV

Clouds of amber, dreams of gladness,
  Dulcet joys and sports of youth,
Soon must yield to haughty sadness;
  Mercy holds the veil to Truth.

V

See Erostratus the second
  Fires again Diana's fane;
By the Fates from Orcus beckon'd,
  Clouds envelop Drury Lane.

VI

Lurid smoke and frank suspicion
  Hand in hand reluctant dance:
While the God fulfils his mission,
  Chivalry, resign thy lance.

VII

Hark! the engines blandly thunder,
  Fleecy clouds dishevell'd lie,
And the firemen, mute with wonder,
  On the son of Saturn cry.

VIII

See the bird of Ammon sailing,
  Perches on the engine's peak,
And, the Eagle firemen hailing,
  Soothes them with its bickering beak.

IX

Juno saw, and mad with malice,
  Lost the prize that Paris gave:
Jealousy's ensanguined chalice,
  Mantling pours the orient wave.

X

Pan beheld Patroclus dying,
  Nox to Niobe was turn'd;
From Busiris Bacchus flying,
  Saw his Semele inurn'd.

XI

Thus fell Drury's lofty glory,
  Levell'd with the shuddering stones;
Mars, with tresses black and gory,
  Drinks the dew of pearly groans.

XII

Hark! what soft Eolian numbers
  Gem the blushes of the morn!

Mrs Robinson

DRURY'S DIRGE

Break, Amphion, break your slumbers,
   Nature's ringlets deck the thorn.

XIII

Ha! I hear the strain erratic
   Dimly glance from pole to pole;
Raptures sweet and dreams ecstatic
   Fire my everlasting soul.

XIV

Where is Cupid's crimson motion?
   Billowy ecstasy of woe,
Bear me straight, meandering ocean,
   Where the stagnant torrents flow.

XV

Blood in every vein is gushing,
   Vixen vengeance lulls my heart;
See, the Gorgon gang is rushing!
   Never, never let us part!

A TALE OF DRURY LANE
BY W. S.

" Thus he went on, stringing one extravagance upon another, in the style his books of chivalry had taught him, and imitating, as near as he could, their very phrase."   DON QUIXOTE.

[To be spoken by Mr. Kemble, in a suit of the Black Prince's Armour, borrowed from the Tower.]

S U R V E Y this shield, all bossy bright—
These cuisses twain behold!
Look on my form in armour dight
Of steel inlaid with gold;
My knees are stiff in iron buckles,
Stiff spikes of steel protect my knuckles.
These once belong'd to sable prince,
Who never did in battle wince;
With valour tart as pungent quince,
   He slew the vaunting Gaul.
Rest there awhile, my bearded lance,
While from green curtain I advance
To yon foot-lights, no trivial dance,
And tell the town what sad mischance
   Did Drury Lane befall.

THE NIGHT
On fair Augusta's towers and trees
Flitted the silent midnight breeze,
Curling the foliage as it past,

Walter Scott

A TALE OF DRURY LANE

Which from the moon-tipp'd plumage cast
A spangled light, like dancing spray,
Then reassumed its still array;
When, as night's lamp unclouded hung,
And down its full effulgence flung,
It shed such soft and balmy power
That cot and castle, hall and bower,
And spire and dome, and turret height,
Appear'd to slumber in the light.
From Henry's chapel, Rufus' hall,
To Savoy, Temple, and St. Paul,
From Knightsbridge, Pancras, Camden Town,
To Redriff, Shadwell, Horsleydown,
No voice was heard, no eye unclosed,
But all in deepest sleep reposed.
They might have thought, who gazed around
Amid a silence so profound,
    It made the senses thrill,
That 'twas no place inhabited,
But some vast city of the dead—
    All was so hush'd and still.

The Burning

As Chaos, which, by heavenly doom,
Had slept in everlasting gloom,
Started with terror and surprise
When light first flash'd upon her eyes—
So London's sons in nightcap woke,
    In bed-gown woke her dames;
For shouts were heard 'mid fire and smoke,
And twice ten hundred voices spoke—
    "The playhouse is in flames!"
And, lo! where Catherine Street extends,
A fiery tail its lustre lends

To every window-pane;
Blushes each spout in Martlet Court,
And Barbican, moth-eaten fort,
And Covent Garden kennels sport,
　　A bright ensanguined drain;
Meux's new brewhouse shews the light,
Rowland Hill's chapel, and the height
　　Where patent shot they sell;
The Tennis Court, so fair and tall,
Partakes the ray, with Surgeons' Hall,
The ticket-porters' house of call,
Old Bedlam, close by London Wall,
Wright's shrimp and oyster shop withal,
　　And Richardson's Hotel.
Nor these alone, but far and wide,
Across red Thames's gleaming tide,
To distant fields, the blaze was borne,
And daisy white and hoary thorne
In borrow'd lustre seem'd to sham
The rose or red sweet Wil-li-am.
To those who on the hills around
Beheld the flames from Drury's mound,
　　As from a lofty altar rise,
It seem'd that nations did conspire
To offer to the god of fire
　　Some vast stupendous sacrifice!
The summon'd firemen woke at call,
And hied them to their stations all:
Starting from short and broken snooze,
Each sought his pond'rous hobnail'd shoes,
But first his worsted hosen plied,
Plush breeches next, in crimson died,
　　His nether bulk embraced;
Then jacket thick, of red or blue,

A TALE OF DRURY LANE

Whose massý shoulder gave to view
The badge of each respective crew,
    In tin or copper traced.
The engines thunder'd through the street,
Fire-hook, pipe, bucket, all complete,
And torches glared, and clattering feet
    Along the pavement paced.
And one, the leader of the band,
From Charing Cross along the Strand,
Like stag by beagles hunted hard,
Ran till he stopp'd at Vin'gar Yard.
The burning badge his shoulder bore,
The belt and oil-skin hat he wore,
The cane he had, his men to bang,
Show'd foreman of the British gang—
His name was Higginbottom. Now
'Tis meet that I should tell you how
    The others came in view:
The Hand-in-Hand the race begun,
Then came the Phœnix and the Sun,
Th' Exchange, where old insurers run,
    The Eagle, where the new;
With these came Rumford, Bumford, Cole,
Robins from Hockly in the Hole,
Lawson and Dawson, cheek by jowl,
    Crump from St. Giles's Pound:
Whitford and Mitford join'd the train,
Huggins and Muggins from Chick Lane,
And Clutterbuck, who got a sprain
    Before the plug was found.
Hobson and Jobson did not sleep,
But ah! no trophy could they reap,
For both were in the Donjon Keep
    Of Bridewell's gloomy mound

E'en Higginbottom now was posed,
For sadder scene was ne'er disclosed;
Without, within, in hideous show,
Devouring flames resistless glow,
And blazing rafters downward go,
And never halloo " Heads below! "
    Nor notice give at all.
The firemen terrified are slow
To bid the pumping torrent flow,
    For fear the roof should fall.
Back, Robins, back! Crump, stand aloof!
    Whitford, keep near the walls!
Huggins, regard your own behoof,
For, lo! the blazing rocking roof
    Down, down, in thunder falls!
An awful pause succeeds the stroke,
And o'er the ruins volumed smoke,
Rolling around its pitchy shroud,
Conceal'd them from th' astonish'd crowd.
At length the mist awhile was clear'd,
When, lo! amid the wreck uprear'd,
Gradual a moving head appear'd,
    And Eagle firemen knew
'Twas Joseph Muggins, name revered,
    The foreman of their crew.
Loud shouted all in signs of wo,
" A Muggins! to the rescue, ho! "
    And pour'd the hissing tide:
Meanwhile the Muggins fought amain,
And strove and struggled all in vain,
For, rallying but to fall again,
    He totter'd, sunk, and died!

Did none attempt, before he fell,

A TALE OF DRURY LANE

To succour one they loved so well?
Yes, Higginbottom did aspire
(His fireman's soul was all on fire),
    His brother chief to save;

But ah! his reckless generous ire
    Served but to share his grave!
Mid blazing beams and scalding streams,
Through fire and smoke he dauntless broke,
    Where Muggins broke before.
But sulphury stench and boiling drench

Destroying sight o'erwhelm'd him quite,
    He sunk to rise no more.
Still o'er his head, while Fate he braved,
His whizzing water-pipe he waved;
" Whitford and Mitford, ply your pumps,
" You, Clutterbuck, come, stir your stumps,
" Why are you in such doleful dumps?
" A fireman, and afraid of bumps!—
" What are they fear'd on? fools! 'od rot 'em! "
Were the last words of Higginbottom.

The Revival

Peace to his soul! new prospects bloom,
And toil rebuilds what fires consume!
Eat we and drink we, be our ditty,
" Joy to the managing committee! "
Eat we and drink we, join to rum
Roast beef and pudding of the plum;
Forth from thy nook, John Horner, come,
With bread of ginger brown thy thumb,
    For this is Drury's gay day:
Roll, roll thy hoop, and twirl thy tops,
And buy, to glad thy smiling chops,
Crisp parliament with lollypops,
    And fingers of the Lady.

Didst mark, how toil'd the busy train,
From morn to eve, till Drury Lane
Leap'd like a roebuck from the plain?
Ropes rose and sunk, and rose again,
    And nimble workmen trod;
To realise bold Wyatt's plan
Rush'd many a howling Irishman;
Loud clatter'd many a porter-can,

A TALE OF DRURY LANE

And many a ruggamuffin clan,
    With trowel and with hod.

Drury revives! her rounded pate
Is blue, is heavenly blue with slate;
She " wings the midway air " elate,
    As magpie, crow, or chough;
White paint her modish visage smears,
Yellow and pointed are her ears,
No pendant portico appears
Dangling beneath, for Whitbread's shears
    Have cut the bauble off.

Yes, she exalts her stately head;
And, but that solid bulk outspread,
Opposed you on your onward tread,
And posts and pillars warranted
That all was true that Wyatt said,
You might have deem'd her walls so thick
Were not composed of stone or brick,
But all a phantom, all a trick,
Of brain disturb'd and fancy-sick,
So high she soars, so vast, so quick!

JOHNSON'S GHOST

[*Ghost of Dr.* JOHNSON *rises from trap-door P. S., and Ghost of* BOSWELL *from trap-door O. P. The latter bows respectfully to the House, and obsequiously to the Doctor's Ghost, and retires.*]

Doctor's Ghost loquitur

T H A T which was organised by the moral ability of one has been executed by the physical efforts of many, and DRURY LANE THEATRE is now complete. Of that part behind the curtain, which has not yet been destined to glow beneath the brush of the varnisher, or vibrate to the hammer of the carpenter, little is thought by the public, and little need be said by the committee. Truth, however, is not to be sacrificed for the accommodation of either; and he who should pronounce that our edifice has received its final embellishment would be disseminating falsehood without incurring favour, and risking the disgrace of detection without participating the advantage of success.

Professions lavishly effused and parsimoniously verified are alike inconsistent with the precepts of innate rectitude and the practice of external policy: let it not then be conjectured, that because we are unassuming, we are imbecile; that forbearance is any indication of despondency, or humility of demerit. He that is the most assured of success will make the fewest appeals to favour, and where nothing is claimed that is undue, nothing that is due will be withheld. A swelling opening is too often succeeded by an insignificant con-

Samuel Johnson LLD

clusion. Parturiént mountains have ere now produced muscipular abortions; and the auditor who compares incipient grandeur with final vulgarity is reminded of the pious hawkers of Constantinople, who solemnly perambulate her streets, exclaiming, " In the name of the Prophet—figs! "

Of many who think themselves wise, and of some who are thought wise by others, the exertions are directed to the revival of mouldering and obscure dramas; to endeavours to exalt that which is now rare only because it was always worthless, and whose deterioration, while it condemned it to living obscurity, by a strange obliquity of moral perception constitutes its title to posthumous renown. To embody the flying colours of folly, to arrest evanescence, to give to bubbles the globular consistency as well as form, to exhibit on the stage the piebald denizen of the stable, and the half-reasoning parent of combs, to display the brisk locomotion of Columbine, or the tortuous attitudenising of Punch;—these are the occupations of others, whose ambition, limited to the applause of unintellectual fatuity, is too innocuous for the application of satire, and too humble for the incitement of jealousy.

Our refectory will be found to contain every species of fruit, from the cooling nectarine and luscious peach to the puny pippin and the noxious nut. There Indolence may repose, and Inebriety revel; and the spruce apprentice, rushing in at second account, may there chatter with impunity; debarred, by a barrier of brick and mortar, from marring that scenic interest in others, which nature and education have disqualified him from comprehending himself.

Permanent stage-doors we have none. That which is permanent cannot be removed, for, if removed, it soon ceases to be permanent. What stationary absurdity can vie with that ligneous barricado, which, decorated with frappant and tintinnabulant appendages, now serves as the entrance of the lowly cottage, and now as the exit of a lady's bed-chamber; at one time, insinuating plastic Harlequin into a butcher's shop, and, at another, yawning, as a flood-gate, to precipitate the Cyprians of St. Giles's into the embraces of Macheath. To elude this glaring absurdity, to give to each respective mansion the door which the carpenter would doubtless have given, we vary our portal with the varying scene, passing from deal to mahogany, and from mahogany to oak, as the opposite claims of cottage, palace, or castle may appear to require.

Amid the general hum of gratulation which flatters us in front, it is fit that some regard should be paid to the murmurs of despondence that assail us in the rear. They, as I have elsewhere expressed it, " who live to please," should not have their own pleasures entirely overlooked. The children of Thespis are general in their censures of the architect, in having placed the locality of exit at such a distance from the oily irradiators which now dazzle the eyes of him who addresses you. I am, cries the Queen of Terrors, robbed of my fair proportions. When the king-killing Thane hints to the breathless auditory the murders he means to perpetrate, in the castle of Macduff, "ere his purpose cool"; so vast is the interval he has to travel before he can escape from the stage, that his purpose has even time to freeze. Your condition, cries the Muse of Smiles, is hard, but it is cygnet's down in comparison with mine. The peerless peer of capers and congees has laid it down as a rule, that the best good thing uttered by the morning visitor should conduct him rapidly to the

JOHNSON'S GHOST

doorway, last impressions vying in durability with first. But when, on this boarded elongation, it falls to my lot to say a good thing, to ejaculate, " keep moving." or to chant, " *hic hoc horum genitivo*," many are the moments that must elapse, ere I can hide myself from public vision in the recesses of O. P. or P. S.

To objections like these, captiously urged and querulously maintained, it is time that equity should conclusively reply. Deviation from scenic propriety has only to vituperate itself for the consequences it generates. Let the actor consider the line of exit as that line beyond which he should not soar in quest of spurious applause: let him reflect, that in proportion as he advances to the lamps, he recedes from nature; that the truncheon of Hotspur acquires no additional charm from encountering the cheek of beauty in the stage-box, and that the bravura of Mandane may produce effect, although the throat of her who warbles it should not overhang the orchestra. The Jove of the modern critical Olympus, Lord Mayor of the theatric sky, has, *ex cathedrâ*, asserted, that a natural actor looks upon the audience part of the theatre as the third side of the chamber he inhabits. Surely, of the third wall thus fancifully erected, our actors should, by ridicule or reason, be withheld from knocking their heads against the stucco.

Time forcibly reminds me that all things which have a limit must be brought to a conclusion. Let me, ere that conclusion arrives, recall to your recollection, that the pillars which rise on either side of me, blooming in virid antiquity, like two massy evergreens, had yet slumbered in their native quarry, but for the ardent exertions of the individual who called them into life: to his never-slumbering talents you are indebted for whatever pleasure this haunt of the muses is calculated to afford. If, in defiance of chaotic malevolence, the destroyer of the temple of Diana yet survives in the name of Erostratus, surely we may confidently predict, that the rebuilder of the temple of Apollo will stand recorded to distant posterity in that of—SAMUEL WHITBREAD.

THE BEAUTIFUL INCENDIARY
BY THE HON. W. S.

Formosam resonare doces Amaryllida silvas.
VIRGIL.

Scene draws, and discovers a Lady asleep on a couch.
Enter PHILANDER

PHILANDER

I

S O B R I E T Y, cease to be sober,
   Cease, Labour, to dig and to delve;
All hail to this tenth of October,
   One thousand eight hundred and twelve!
Ha! whom do my peepers remark?
   'Tis Hebe with Jupiter's jug;
O no, 'tis the pride of the Park,
   Fair Lady Elizabeth Mugg.

II

Why, beautiful nymph, do you close
   The curtain that fringes your eye?
Why veil in the clouds of repose
   The sun that should brighten our sky?
Perhaps jealous Venus has oiled
   Your hair with some opiate drug,
Not choosing her charms should be foiled
   By Lady Elizabeth Mugg.

III

But ah! why awaken the blaze
   Those bright burning-glasses contain
Whose lens with concentrated rays
   Proved fatal to old Drury Lane?
'Twas all accidental they cry,—
   Away with the flimsy humbug!
'Twas fired by a flash from the eye
   Of Lady Elizabeth Mugg.

IV

Thy glance can in us raise a flame,
   Then why should old Drury be free?
Our doom and its dome are the same,
   Both subject to beauty's decree.
No candles the workmen consumed,
   When deep in the ruins they dug;
Thy flash still their progress illumed,
   Sweet Lady Elizabeth Mugg.

V

Thy face a rich fire-place displays:
   The mantel-piece marble—thy brows;
Thine eye, are the bright beaming blaze;
   Thy bib, which no trespass allows,
The fender's tall barrier marks;
   Thy tippet's the fire-quelling rug,
Which serves to extinguish the sparks
   Of Lady Elizabeth Mugg.

VI

The Countess a lily appears,
   Whose tresses the pearl-drops emboss

THE BEAUTIFUL INCENDIARY

  The Marchioness, blooming in years,
    A rose-bud enveloped in moss;
  But thou art the sweet passion-flower,
    For who would not slavery hug,
  To pass but one exquisite hour
    In the arms of Elizabeth Mugg?

VII

  When at court, or some Dowager's rout,
    Her diamond aigrette meets our view,
  She looks like a glow-worm dressed out,
    Or tulips bespangled with dew.
  Her two lips denied to man's suit,
    Are shared with her favourite Pug;
  What lord would not change with the brute,
    To live with Elizabeth Mugg?

VIII

  Could the stage be a large vis-à-vis,
    Reserved for the polished and great,
  Where each happy lover might see
    The nymph he adores tête-à-tête;
  No longer I'd gaze on the ground,
    And the load of despondency lug,
  For I'd book myself all the year round,
    To ride with the sweet Lady Mugg.

IX

  Yes, she in herself is a host,
    And if she were here all alone,
  Our house might nocturnally boast
    A bumper of fashion and ton.

REJECTED ADDRESSES

Again should it burst in a blaze,
   In vain would they ply Congreve's plug,
For nought could extinguish the rays
   From the glance of divine Lady Mugg.

X

O could I as Harlequin frisk,
   And thou be my Columbine fair,
My wand should with one magic whisk
   Transport us to Hanover Square:
St. George's should lend us its shrine,
   The parson his shoulders might shrug,
But a license should force him to join
   My hand in the hand of my Mugg.

XI

Court-plaster the weapons should tip,
   By Cupid shot down from above,
Which, cut into spots for thy lip,
   Should still barb the arrows of love.
The god who from others flies quick,
   With us should be slow as a slug;
As close as a leech he should stick
   To me and Elizabeth Mugg.

XII

For Time would, with us, 'stead of sand,
   Put filings of steel in his glass,
To dry up the blots of his hand,
   And spangle life's page as they pass.
Since all flesh is grass ere 'tis hay,
   O may I in clover live snug,
And when old Time mows me away,
   Be stacked with defunct Lady Mugg!

FIRE AND ALE

BY M. G. L.

Omnia transformat sese in miracula rerum.
VIRG.

My palate is parched with Pierian thirst,
    Away to Parnassus I'm beckoned;
List, warriors and dames, while my lay is rehearsed
I sing of the singe of Miss Drury the first,
    And the birth of Miss Drury the second.

The Fire King, one day, rather amorous felt;
    He mounted his hot copper filly;
His breeches and boots were of tin, and the belt
Was made of cast iron, for fear it should melt
    With the heat of the copper colt's belly.

Sure never was skin half so scalding as his!
    When an infant 'twas equally horrid;
For the water, when he was baptised, gave a fizz,
And bubbled and simmer'd and started off, whizz!
    As soon as it sprinkled his forehead.

Oh! then there was glitter and fire in each eye,
    For two living coals were the symbols;
His teeth were calcined, and his tongue was so dry,
It rattled against them, as though you should try
    To play the piano in thimbles.

From his nostrils a lava sulphureous flows,
    Which scorches wherever it lingers;
A snivelling fellow he's call'd by his foes,
For he can't raise his paw up to blow his red nose,
    For fear it should blister his fingers.

His wig is of flames curling over his head,
    Well powder'd with white smoking ashes;
He drinks gunpowder tea, melted sugar of lead,
Cream of tartar, and dines on hot spice gingerbread,
    Which black from the oven he gnashes.

Each fire nymph his kiss from her countenance shields,
    'Twould soon set her cheekbone a frying;
He spit in the tenter ground near Spital-fields,
And the hole that it burnt, and the chalk that it yields,
    Make a capital lime-kiln for drying.

When he open'd his mouth, out there issued a blast,
    (Nota bene, I do not mean swearing),
But the noise that it made, and the heat that it cast,
I've heard it from those who have seen it, surpass'd
    A shot manufactory flaring.

He blazed, and he blazed, as he gallop'd to snatch
    His bride, little dreaming of danger;
His whip was a torch, and his spur was a match,
And over the horse's left eye was a patch,
    To keep it from burning the manger.

And who is the housemaid he means to enthral
    In his cinder-producing alliance?
'Tis Drury-Lane Playhouse, so wide, and so tall,
Who, like other combustible ladies, must fall,
    If she cannot set sparks at defiance.

M. G. LEWIS

FIRE AND ALE

On his warming-pan kneepan he clattering roll'd,
    And the housemaid his hand would have taken,
But his hand, like his passion, was too hot to hold,
And she soon let it go, but her new ring of gold
    All melted, like butter or bacon!

Oh! then she look'd sour, and indeed well she might,
    For Vinegar Yard was before her;
But, spite of her shrieks, the ignipotent knight,
Enrobing the maid in a flame of gas light,
    To the skies in a sky-rocket bore her.

Look! look! 'tis the Ale King, so stately and starch,
    Whose votaries scorn to be sober;
He pops from his vat, like a cedar or larch;
Brown-stout is his doublet, he hops in his march,
    And froths at the mouth in October.

His spear is a spigot, his shield is a bung;
    He taps where the housemaid no more is,
When lo! at his magical bidding, upsprung
A second Miss Drury, tall, tidy, and young,
    And sported *in loco sororis.*

Back, lurid in air, for a second regale,
    The Cinder King, hot with desire,
To Brydges Street hied; but the Monarch of Ale,
With uplifted spigot and faucet, and pail,
    Thus chided the Monarch of Fire:

" Vile tyrant, beware of the ferment I brew;
    " I rule the roast here, dash the wig o' me!
" If, spite of your marriage with Old Drury, you
" Come here with your tinderbox, courting the New,
    " I'll have you indicted for bigamy! "

PLAYHOUSE MUSINGS
BY S. T. C.

   Ille velut fidis arcana sodalibus olim
    Credebat libris; neque si male cesserat, usquam
    Decurrens alio, neque si bene.   HOR.

MY pensive Public, wherefore look you sad?
I had a grandmother, she kept a donkey
To carry to the mart her crockery ware,
And when that donkey look'd me in the face,
His face was sad! and you are sad, my Public!

   Joy should be yours: this tenth day of October
Again assembles us in Drury Lane.
Long wept my eye to see the timber planks
That hid our ruins; many a day I cried,
Ah me! I fear they never will rebuild it!
Till on one eve, one joyful Monday eve,
As along Charles Street I prepared to walk,
Just at the corner, by the pastrycook's,
I heard a trowel tick against a brick.
I look'd me up, and straight a parapet
Uprose at least seven inches o'er the planks.
Joy to thee, Drury! to myself I said:
He of Blackfriars' Road, who hymn'd thy downfall
In loud Hosannahs, and who prophesied
That flames, like those from prostrate Solyma,
Would scorch the hand that ventured to rebuild thee,
Has proved a lying prophet. From that hour,

Samuel Taylor Coleridge

PLAYHOUSE MUSINGS

As leisure offer'd, close to Mr. Spring's
Box-office door, I've stood and eyed the builders.
They had a plan to render less their labours;
Workmen in olden times would mount a ladder
With hodded heads, but these stretch'd forth a pole
From the wall's pinnacle, they placed a pulley
Athwart the pole, a rope athwart the pulley;
To this a basket dangled; mortar and bricks
Thus freighted, swung securely to the top,
And in the empty basket workmen twain
Precipitate, unhurt, accosted earth.

Oh! 'twas a goodly sound, to hear the people
Who watch'd the work, express their various thoughts!
While some believed it never would be finish'd,
Some, on the contrary, believed it would.

I've heard our front that faces Drury Lane
Much criticised; they say 'tis vulgar brick-work,
A mimic manufactory of floor-cloth.
One of the morning papers wish'd that front
Cemented like the front in Brydges-Street;
As it now looks, they call it Wyatt's Mermaid,
A handsome woman with a fish's tail.

White is the steeple of St. Bride's in Fleet-Street;
The Albion (as its name denotes) is white;
Morgan and Saunders' shop for chairs and tables
Gleams like a snow-ball in the setting sun;
White is Whitehall. But not St. Bride's in Fleet-Street,
The spotless Albion, Morgan, no, nor Saunders,
Nor white Whitehall, is white as Drury's face.

Oh, Mr. Whitbread! fie upon you, sir!
I think you should have built a colonnade;
When tender Beauty, looking for her coach,
Protrudes her gloveless hand, perceives the shower,
And draws the tippet closer round her throat,
Perchance her coach stands half a dozen off,
And, ere she mounts the step, the oozing mud
Soaks through her pale kid slipper. On the morrow,
She coughs at breakfast, and her gruff papa
Cries, " There you go! this comes of playhouses! "
To build no portico is penny wise:
Heaven grant it prove not in the end pound foolish!

Hail to thee, Drury! Queen of Theatres!
What is the Regency in Tottenham Street,
The Royal Amphitheatre of Arts,
Astley's, Olympic, or the Sans Pareil,
Compar'd with thee? Yet when I view thee push'd
Back from the narrow street that christen'd thee,
I know not why they call thee Drury Lane.

Amid the freaks that modern fashion sanctions,
It grieves me much to see live animals
Brought on the stage. Grimaldi has his rabbit,
Laurent his cat, and Bradbury his pig;
Fie on such tricks! Johnson, the machinist
Of former Drury, imitated life
Quite to the life. The elephant in Blue Beard,
Stuff'd by his hand, wound round his lithe proboscis,
As spruce as he who roar'd in Padmanaba.
Nought born on earth should die. On hackney stands
I reverence the coachman who cries " Gee,"
And spares the lash. When I behold a spider

PLAYHOUSE MUSINGS

Prey on a fly, a magpie on a worm,
Or view a butcher with horn-handled knife
Slaughter a tender lamb as dead as mutton,
Indeed, indeed, I'm very, very sick!
       [Exit hastily.

DRURY LANE HUSTINGS
A NEW HALFPENNY BALLAD
BY A PIC NIC POET

This is the very age of promise: To promise is most courtly and fashionable. Performance is a kind of will or testament, which argues a great sickness in his judgment that makes it.
TIMON OF ATHENS.

[*To be sung by Mr.* JOHNSTONE *in the character of*
LOONEY M'TWOLTER]

I

M R . J A C K , your address, says the Prompter to me,
So I gave him my card—no, that a'nt it, says he;
'Tis your public address. Oh! says I, never fear,
If address you are bother'd for, only look here.
[Puts on hat affectedly.
Tol de rol lol, &c.

II

With Drury's for sartin we'll never have done,
We've built up another, and yet there's but one;
The old one was best, yet I'd say, if I durst,
The new one is better—the last is the first.
Tol de rol, &c.

III

These pillars are call'd by a Frenchified word,
A something that's jumbled of antique and verd;

The boxes may show us some verdant antiques,
Some old harridans who beplaster their cheeks.
      Tol de rol, &c.

IV

Only look how high Tragedy, Comedy, stick,
Lest their rivals, the horses, should give them a kick!
If you will not descend when our authors beseech ye,
You'll stop there for life, for I'm sure they can't reach ye.
      Tol de rol, &c.

V

Each one shilling god within reach of a nod is,
And plain are the charms of each gallery goddess—
You, Brandy-faced Moll, don't be looking askew,
When I talk'd of a goddess I didn't mean you.
      Tol de rol, &c.

VI

Our stage is so prettily fashion'd for viewing,
The whole house can see what the whole house is doing:
'Tis just like the Hustings, we kick up a bother;
But saying is one thing, and doing's another.
      Tol de rol, &c.

VII

We've many new houses, and some of them rum ones,
But the newest of all is the new House of Commons;
'Tis a rickety sort of a bantling, I'm told,
It will die of old age when it's seven years old.
      Tol de rol, &c.

VIII

As I don't know on whom the election will fall,
I move in return for returning them all;
But for fear Mr. Speaker my meaning should miss,
The house that I wish 'em to sit in is this.
       Tol de rol, &c.

IX

Let us cheer our great Commoner, but for whose aid
We all should have gone with short commons to bed;
And since he has saved all the fat from the fire,
I move that the house be call'd Whitbread's Entire.
       Tol de rol, &c.

ARCHITECTURAL ATOMS

TRANSLATED BY DR. B.

Lege, Dick, Lege!   JOSEPH ANDREWS.

To be recited by the Translator's Son

A w a y, fond dupes! who, smit with sacred lore,
Mosaic dreams in Genesis explore,
Doat with Copernicus, or darkling stray
With Newton, Ptolemy, or Tycho Brahe!

To you I sing not, for I sing of truth,
Primeval systems, and creation's youth;
Such as of old, with magic wisdom fraught,
Inspired Lucretius to the Latians taught.

I sing how casual bricks, in airy climb,
Encounter'd casual cow-hair, casual lime;
How rafters, borne through wondering clouds elate,
Kiss'd in their slope blue elemental slate,
Clasp'd solid beams in chance-directed fury,
And gave to birth our renovated Drury.

Thee, son of Jove! whose sceptre was confess'd,
Where fair Æolia springs from Tethys' breast;
Thence on Olympus, mid celestials placed,
God of the Winds, and Ether's boundless waste—
Thee I invoke! Oh *puff* my bold design,
Prompt the bright thought, and swell th' harmonious line;
Uphold my pinions, and my verse inspire
With Winsor's patent gas, or wind of fire,
In whose pure blaze thy embryo form enroll'd,
The dark enlightens, and enchafes the cold.

But, while I court thy gifts, be mine to shun
The deprecated prize Ulysses won;
Who, sailing homeward from thy breezy shore,
The prison'd winds in skins of parchment bore.
Speeds the fleet bark, till o'er the billowy green
The azure heights of Ithaca are seen;
But while with favouring gales her way she wins,
His curious comrades ope the mystic skins;
When, lo! the rescued winds, with boisterous sweep,
Roar to the clouds and lash the rocking deep;

Dr. Busby.

ARCHITECTURAL ATOMS

Heaves the smofe vessel in the howling blast,
Splits the stretch'd sail, and cracks the tottering mast.
Launch'd on a plank, the buoyant hero rides,
Where ebon Afric stems the sable tides,
While his duck'd comrades o'er the ocean fly,
And sleep not in the whole skins they untie.

So, when to raise the wind some lawyer tries,
Mysterious skins of parchment meet our eyes;
On speeds the smiling suit—" Pleas of our Lord
The King " shine sable on the wide record;
Nods the prunella'd bar, attorneys smile,
And syren jurors flatter to beguile;
Till stript—nonsuited—he is doom'd to toss
In legal shipwreck and redeemless loss!
Lucky, if, like Ulysses, he can keep
His head above the waters of the deep.

Æolian monarch! Emperor of Puffs!
We modern sailors dread not thy rebuffs;
See to thy golden shore promiscuous come
Quacks for the lame, the blind, the deaf, the dumb;
Fools are their bankers—a prolific line,
And every mortal malady's a mine.
Each sly Sangrado, with his poisonous pill,
Flies to the printer's devil with his bill,
Whose Midas touch can gild his asses' ears,
And load a knave with folly's rich arrears.
And lo! a second miracle is thine,
For sloe-juice water stands transform'd to wine.
Where Day and Martin's patent blacking roll'd,
Burst from the vase Pactolian streams of gold;
Laugh the sly wizards, glorying in their stealth,
Quit the black art, and loll in lazy wealth.

See Britain's Algerines, the lottery fry,
Win annual tribute by the annual lie!
Aided by thee—but whither do I stray?—
Court, city, borough, own thy sovereign sway;
An age of puffs an age of gold succeeds,
And windy bubbles are the spawn it breeds.

If such thy power, O hear the Muse's prayer!
Swell thy loud lungs and wave thy wings of air;
Spread, viewless giant, all thy arms of mist
Like windmill-sails to bring the poet grist;
As erst thy roaring son, with eddying gale,
Whirl'd Orithyia from her native vale—
So, while Lucretian wonders I rehearse,
Augusta's sons shall patronise my verse.

I sing of ATOMS, whose creative brain,
With edding impulse, built new Drury Lane;
Not to the labours of subservient man,
To no young Wyatt appertains the plan—
We mortals stalk, like horses in a mill,
Impassive media of atomic will;
Ye stare! then Truth's broad talisman discern--
'Tis Demonstration speaks—attend, and learn!

From floating elements in chaos hurl'd,
Self-form'd of atoms, sprang the infant world:
No great *First Cause* inspired the happy plot,
But all was matter—and no matter what.
Atoms, attracted by some law occult,
Settling in spheres, the globe was the result:
Pure child of *Chance*, which still directs the ball,
As rotatory atoms rise or fall.
In ether launch'd, the peopled bubble floats,

ARCHITECTURAL ATOMS

A mass of particles and confluent motes,
So nicely poised, that if one atom flings
Its weight away, aloft the planet springs,
And wings its course through realms of boundless space,
Outstripping comets in eccentric race.
Add but one atom more, it sinks outright
Down to the realms of Tartarus and night.
What waters melt or scorching fires consume,
In different forms their being reassume:
Hence can no change arise, except in name,
For weight and substance ever are the same.

   Thus with the flames that from old Drury rise
Its elements primeval sought the skies;
There pendulous to wait the happy hour
When new attractions should restore their power:
So, in this procreant theatre elate,
Echoes unborn their future life await;
Here embryo sounds in ether lie conceal'd,
Like words in northern atmosphere congeal'd.
Here many a fœtus laugh and half encore
Clings to the roof, or creeps along the floor;
By puffs concipient some in ether flit,
And soar in bravos from the thundering pit;
Some forth on ticket-nights from tradesmen break,
To mar the actor they design to make;
While some this mortal life abortive miss,
Crush'd by a groan, or strangled by a hiss.
So, when " Dog's-meat " re-echoes through the streets,
Rush sympathetic dogs from their retreats,
Beam with bright blaze their supplicating eyes,
Sink their hind-legs, ascend their joyful cries;
Each, wild with hope, and maddening to prevail,
Points the pleased ear, and wags the expectant tail.

REJECTED ADDRESSES

Ye fallen bricks! in Drury's fire calcined,
Since doom'd to slumber, couch'd upon the wind,
Sweet was the hour, when, tempted by your freaks,
Congenial trowels smooth'd your yellow cheeks.
Float dulcet serenades upon the ear,
Bends every atom from its ruddy sphere,
Twinkles each eye, and, peeping from its veil,
Marks in the adverse crowd its destined male.
The oblong beauties clap their hands of grit,
And brick-dust titterings on the breezes flit;
Then down they rush in amatory race,
Their dusty bridegrooms eager to embrace.
Some choose old lovers, some decide for new,
But each, when fix'd, is to her station true.
Thus various bricks are made, as tastes invite—
The red, the gray, the dingy, or the white.

Perhaps some half-baked rover, frank and free,
To alien beauty bends the lawless knee,
But of unhallow'd fascinations sick,
Soon quits his Cyprian for his married brick;
The Dido atom calls and scolds in vain,
No crisp Æneas soothes the widow's pain.

So in Cheapside, what time Aurora peeps,
A mingled noise of dustmen, milk, and sweeps,
Falls on the housemaid's ear: amazed she stands,
Then opes the door with cinder-sabled hands,
And " Matches " calls. The dustman, bubbled flat,
Thinks 'tis for him, and doffs his fan-tail'd hat;
The milkman, whom her second cries assail,
With sudden sink unyokes the clinking pail;
Now louder grown, by turns she screams and weeps—
Alas! her screaming only brings the sweeps.

ARCHITECTURAL ATOMS

Sweeps but put out—she wants to raise a flame,
And calls for matches, but 'tis still the same.
Atoms and housemaids! mark the moral true—
If once ye go astray, no *match* for you!

   As atoms in one mass united mix,
So bricks attraction feel for kindred bricks;
Some in the cellar view, perchance, on high,
Fair chimney chums on beds of mortar lie;
Enamour'd of the sympathetic clod,
Leaps the red bridegroom to the labourer's hod;
And up the ladder bears the workman, taught
To think he bears the bricks—mistaken thought!
A proof behold: if near the top they find
The nymphs or broken-corner'd or unkind,
Back to the base, " resulting with a bound,"
They bear their bleeding carriers to the ground!

   So legends tell along the lofty hill
Paced the twin heroes, gallant Jack and Jill;
On trudged the Gemini to reach the rail
That shields the well's top from the expectant pail,
When, ah! Jack falls; and, rolling in the rear,
Jill feels the attraction of his kindred sphere:
Head over heels begins his toppling track,
Throws sympathetic somersets with Jack,
And at the mountain's base bobbs plump against him,
      whack!
   Ye living atoms, who unconscious sit,
Jumbled by chance in gallery, box, and pit,
For you no Peter opes the fabled door,
No churlish Charon plies the shadowy oar;
Breathe but a space, and Boreas' casual sweep
Shall bear your scatter'd corses o'er the deep,

To gorge the greedy elements, and mix
With water, marl, and clay, and stones, and sticks;
While, charged with fancied souls, sticks, stones, and
    clay,
Shall take your seats, and hiss or clap the play.

  O happy age! when convert Christians read
No sacred writings but the Pagan creed—
O happy age! when, spurning Newton's dreams,
Our poets' sons recite Lucretian themes,
Abjure the idle systems of their youth,
And turn again to atoms and to truth;—
O happier still! when England's dauntless dames,
Awed by no chaste alarms, no latent shames,
The bard's fourth book unblushingly peruse,
And learn the rampant lessons of the stews!

  All hail, Lucretius! renovated sage!
Unfold the modest mystics of thy page;
Return no more to thy sepulchral shelf,
But live, kind bard—that I may live myself!

THEATRICAL ALARM-BELL
BY THE EDITOR OF THE M. P.

"Bounce, Jupiter, bounce!" O'HARA.

LADIES AND GENTLEMEN,
As it is now the universally-admitted, and indeed pretty-generally-suspected, aim of Mr. Whitbread and the infamous, bloodthirsty, and, in fact, illiberal faction to which he belongs, to burn to the ground this free and happy Protestant city, and establish himself in St. James's Palace, his fellow committee-men have thought it their duty to watch the principles of a theatre built under his auspices. The information they have received from undoubted authority—particularly from an old fruit-woman who has turned king's evidence, and whose name, for obvious reasons, we forbear to mention, though we have had it some weeks in our possession—has induced them to introduce various reforms—not such reforms as the vile faction clamour for, meaning thereby revolution, but such reforms as are necessary to preserve the glorious constitution of the only free, happy, and prosperous country now left upon the face of the earth. From the valuable and authentic source above alluded to, we have learnt that a sanguinary plot has been formed by some united Irishmen, combined with a gang of Luddites, and a special committee sent over by the Pope at the instigation of the beastly Corsican fiend, for destroying all the loyal part of the audience on the anniversary of that

deeply-to-be-abhorred and highly-to-be-blamed stratagem, the Gunpowder Plot, which falls this year on Thursday the 5th of November. The whole is under the direction of a delegated committee of O. P.'s, whose treasonable exploits at Covent Garden you all recollect, and all of whom would have been hung from the chandeliers at that time, but for the mistaken lenity of government. At a given signal, a well-known O. P. was to cry out from the gallery, " Nosey! Music! " whereupon all the O. P.'s were to produce from their inside pockets a long pair of shears, edged with felt, to prevent their making any noise, manufactured expressly by a wretch at Birmingham, one of Mr. Brougham's evidences, and now in custody. With these they were to cut off the heads of all the loyal N. P.'s in the house, without distinction of sex or age. At the signal, similarly given, of " Throw him over! " which it now appears always alluded to the overthrow of our never-sufficiently-enough-to-be-deeply-and-universally-to-be-venerated constitution, all the heads of the N. P.'s were to be thrown at the fiddlers, to prevent their appearing in evidence, or perhaps as a false and illiberal insinuation that they have no heads of their own. All that we know of the further designs of these incendiaries is, that they are by-a-great-deal-too-much too-horrible-to-be-mentioned.

The Manager has acted with his usual promptitude on this trying occasion. He has contracted for 300 tons of gunpowder, which are at this moment placed in a small 'barrel under the pit; and a descendant of Guy Faux, assisted by Col. Congreve, has undertaken to blow up the house, when necessary, in so novel and ingenious a manner, that every O. P. shall be annihilated, while not a whisker of the N. P.'s shall be singed. This strik-

THEATRICAL ALARM-BELL

ingly displays the advantages of loyalty and attachment to government. Several other hints have been taken from the theatrical regulations of the not-a-bit-the-less-on-that-account-to-be-universally-execrated monster Bonaparte. A park of artillery, provided with chain-shot, is to be stationed on the stage, and play upon the audience, in case of any indication of misplaced applause or popular discontent (which accounts for the large space between the curtain and the lamps); and the public will participate our satisfaction in learning that the indecorous custom of standing up with the hat on is to be abolished, as the Bow-street officers are provided with daggers, and have orders to stab all such persons to the heart, and send their bodies to Surgeons' Hall. Gentlemen who cough are only to be slightly wounded. Fruit-women bawling " Bill of the play! " are to be forthwith shot, for which purpose soldiers will be stationed in the slips, and ball-cartridge is to be served out with the lemonade. If any of the spectators happen to sneeze or spit, they are to be transported for life; and any person who is so tall as to prevent another seeing, is to be dragged out and sent on board the tender, or, by an instrument taken out of the pocket of Procrustes, to be forthwith cut shorter, either at the head or foot, according as his own convenience may dictate.

Thus, ladies and gentlemen, have the committee, through my medium, set forth the not-in-a-hurry-to-be paralleled plan they have adopted for preserving order and decorum within the walls of their magnificent edifice. Nor have they, while attentive to their own concerns, by any means overlooked those of the cities of London and Westminster. Finding, on enumeration, that they have with a with-two-hands-and-one-tongue-to-be-applauded liberality, contracted for more gunpowder than they want, they have parted with the surplus to the mattock-carrying and hustings-hammering bailiff of Westminster, who has, with his own shovel, dug a large hole in the front of the parish-church of St. Paul, Covent Garden, that, upon the least symptom of ill-breeding in the mob at the general election, the whole of the market may be blown into the air. This, ladies and gentlemen, may at first make provisions *rise*, but we pledge the credit of our theatre that they will soon *fall* again, and people be supplied, as usual, with vegetables, in the in-general-strewed-with-cabbage-stalks-but-on-Saturday-night-lighted-up-with-lamps market of Covent Garden.

I should expatiate more largely on the other advantages of the glorious constitution of these by-the-whole-of-Europe-envied realms, but I am called away to take an account of the ladies, and other artificial flowers, at a fashionable rout, of which a full and particular account will hereafter appear. For the present, my fashionable intelligence is scanty, on account of the opening of Drury Lane; and the ladies and gentlemen who honour me with their attention will not be surprised if they find nothing under my usual head!!

THE THEATRE
BY THE REV. G. C.

"Nil intentatum nostri liquêre poetæ,
 Nec minimum meruêre decus, vestigia Græca
 Ausi deserere, et celebrare domestica facta."
HOR.

A PREFACE OF APOLOGIES

IF the following poem should be fortunate enough to be selected for the opening address, a few words of explanation may be deemed necessary, on my part, to avert invidious misrepresentation. The animadversion I have thought it right to make on the noise created by tuning the orchestra, will, I hope, give no lasting remorse to any of the gentlemen employed in the band. It is to be desired that they would keep their instruments ready tuned, and strike off at once. This would be an accommodation to many well-meaning persons who frequent the theatre, who, not being blest with the ear of St. Cecilia, mistake the tuning for the overture, and think the latter concluded before it is begun.

"———— one fiddle will
Give, half-ashamed, a tiny flourish still,"

was originally written " one hautboy will; " but, having providentially been informed, when this poem was upon the point of being sent off, that there is but one hautboy in the band, I averted the storm of popular and managerial indignation from the head of its blower:

as it now stands, " one fiddle " among many, the faulty individual will, I hope, escape detection. The story of the flying play-bill is calculated to expose a practice much too common, of pinning play-bills to the cushions insecurely, and frequently, I fear, not pinning them at all. If these lines save one play-bill only from the fate I have recorded, I shall not deem my labour ill employed. The concluding episode of Patrick Jennings' glances at the boorish fashion of wearing the hat in the one-shilling gallery. Had Jennings thrust his between his feet at the commencement of the play, he might have leaned forward with impunity, and the catastrophe I relate would not have occurred. The line of handkerchiefs formed to enable him to recover his loss, is purposely so crossed in texture and materials as to mislead the reader in respect to the real owner of any one of them. For, in the satirical view of life and manners which I occasionally present, my clerical profession has taught me how extremely improper it would be, by any allusion, however slight, to give any uneasiness, however trivial, to any individual, however foolish or wicked. G. C.

THE THEATRE

Interior of a Theatre described.—Pit gradually fills.—The Check-taker.—Pit full.—The Orchestra tuned.—One Fiddle rather dilatory.—Is reproved—and repents.—Evolutions of a Play-bill.—Its final Settlement on the Spikes.—The Gods taken to task—and why.—Motley Group of Play-goers.—Holywell Street, St. Pancras.—Emanuel Jennings binds his Son apprentice—not in London—and why.—Episode of the Hat.

'T I S sweet to view, from half-past five to six,
Our long wax-candles, with short cotton wicks,
Touch'd by the lamplighter's Promethean art,
Start into light, and make the lighter start;
To see red Phœbus through the gallery-pane
Tinge with his beam the beams of Drury Lane;
While gradual parties fill our widen'd pit,
And gape, and gaze, and wonder, ere they sit.

    At first, while vacant seats give choice and ease,
Distant or near, they settle where they please;
But when the multitude contracts the span,
And seats are rare, they settle where they can.

Now the full benches to late-comers doom
No room for standing, miscall'd *standing room*.

    Hark! the check-taker moody silence breaks,
And bawling " Pit full! " gives the check he takes;
Yet onward still the gathering numbers cram,
Contending crowders shout the frequent damn,
And all is bustle, squeeze, row, jabbering, and jam.

    See to their desks Apollo's sons repair—
Swift rides the rosin o'er the horse's hair!
In unison their various tones to tune,
Murmurs the hautboy, growls the hoarse bassoon;
In soft vibration sighs the whispering lute,
Tang goes the harpsichord, too-too the flute,
Brays the loud trumpet, squeaks the fiddle sharp,
Winds the French-horn, and twangs the tingling harp;
Till, like great Jove, the leader, figuring in,
Attunes to order the chaotic din.
Now all seems hush'd—but, no, one fiddle will

Crabbe 1825

THE THEATRE

Give, half-ashamed, a tiny flourish still.
Foil'd in his crash, the leader of the clan
Reproves with frowns the dilatory man:
Then on his candlestick thrice taps his bow,
Nods a new signal, and away they go.

  Perchance, while pit and gallery cry, " Hats off! "
And awed Consumption checks his chided cough,
Some giggling daughter of the Queen of Love
Drops, 'reft of pin, her play-bill from above:
Like Icarus, while laughing galleries clap,
Soars, ducks, and dives in air the printed scrap;
But, wiser far than he, combustion fears,
And, as it flies, eludes the chandeliers;
Till, sinking gradual, with repeated twirl,
It settles, curling, on a fiddler's curl;
Who from his powder'd pate the intruder strikes,
And, for mere malice, sticks it on the spikes.

  Say, why these Babel strains from Babel tongues?
Who's that calls " Silence! " with such leathern lungs?
He who, in quest of quiet, " Silence! " hoots,
Is apt to make the hubbub he imputes.

  What various swains our motley walls contain!—
Fashion from Moorfields, honour from Chick Lane;
Bankers from Paper Buildings here resort,
Bankrupts from Golden Square and Riches Court;
From the Haymarket canting rogues in grain,
Gulls from the Poultry, sots from Water Lane;
The lottery-cormorant, the auction-shark,
The full-price master, and the half-price clerk;
Boys who long linger at the gallery-door,
With pence twice five—they want but twopence more;

Till some Samaritan the twopence spares,
And sends them jumping up the gallery-stairs.

   Critics we boast who ne'er their malice balk,
But talk their minds—we wish they'd mind their talk;
Big-worded bullies, who by quarrels live—
Who give the lie, and tell the lie they give;
Jews from St. Mary Axe, for jobs so wary,
That for old clothes they'd even axe St. Mary;
And bucks with pockets empty as their pate,
Lax in their gaiters, laxer in their gait;
Who oft, when we our house lock up, carouse
With tippling tipstaves in a lock-up house.

   Yet here, as elsewhere, Chance can joy bestow,
Where scowling Fortune seem'd to threaten woe.

   John Richard William Alexander Dwyer
Was footman to Justinian Stubbs, Esquire;
But when John Dwyer listed in the Blues,
Emanuel Jennings polish'd Stubbs's shoes.
Emanuel Jennings brought his youngest boy
Up as a corn-cutter—a safe employ;
In Holywell Street, St. Pancras, he was bred
(At number twenty-seven, it is said),
Facing the pump, and near the Granby's Head:
He would have bound him to some shop in town,
But with a premium he could not come down.
Pat was the urchin's name—a red-hair'd youth,
Fonder of purl and skittle-grounds than truth.

   Silence, ye gods! to keep your tongues in awe,
The Muse shall tell an accident she saw.

THE THEATRE

   Pat Jennings in the upper gallery sat,
But, leaning forward, Jennings lost his hat:
Down from the gallery the beaver flew,
And spurn'd the one to settle in the two.
How shall he act? Pay at the gallery-door
Two shillings for what cost, when new, but four?
Or till half-price, to save his shilling, wait,
And gain his hat again at half-past eight?
Now, while his fears anticipate a thief,
John Mullins whispers, " Take my handkerchief."
" Thank you," cries Pat; " but one won't make a line."
" Take mine," cried Wilson; and cried Stokes, " Take
A motley cable soon Pat Jennings ties,   [mine."
Where Spitalfields with real India vies.
Like Iris' bow, down darts the painted clue,
Starr'd, striped, and spotted, yellow, red, and blue,
Old calico, torn silk, and muslin new.
George Green below, with palpitating hand,
Loops the last 'kerchief to the beaver's band—
Upsoars the prize! The youth, with joy unfeign'd,
Regain'd the felt, and felt what he regain'd;
While to the applauding galleries grateful Pat
Made a low bow, and touch'd the ransom'd hat.

TO THE MANAGING COMMITTEE OF THE NEW DRURY-LANE THEATRE

GENTLEMEN,

Happening to be wool-gathering at the foot of Mount Parnassus, I was suddenly seized with a violent travestie in the head. The first symptoms I felt were several triple rhymes floating about my brain, accompanied by a singing in my throat, which quickly communicated itself to the ears of every body about me, and made me a burthen to my friends and a torment to Doctor Apollo; three of whose favourite servants—that is to say, Macbeth, his butcher; Mrs. Haller, his cook; and George Barnwell, his book-keeper—I waylaid in one of my fits of insanity, and mauled after a very frightful fashion. In this woeful crisis, I accidentally heard of your invaluable New Patent Hissing Pit, which cures every disorder incident to Grub Street. I send you inclosed a more detailed specimen of my case: if you could mould it into the shape of an address, to be said or sung on the first night of your performance, I have no doubt that I should feel the immediate effects of your invaluable New Patent Hissing Pit, of which they tell me one hiss is a dose.   I am, &c.

MOMUS MEDLAR.

CASE, NO. I

MACBETH

[*Enter* MACBETH, *in a red nightcap.* PAGE *following with a torch*]

G o , boy, and thy good mistress tell
  (She knows that my purpose is cruel),
I'd thank her to tingle her bell
  As soon as she's heated my gruel.
Go, get thee to bed and repose—
  To sit up so late is a scandal;
But ere you have ta'en off your clothes,
  Be sure that you put out that candle.
            Ri fol de rol tol de rol lol.

My stars, in the air here's a knife!—
  I'm sure it can not be a hum;
I'll catch at the handle, add's life!
  And then I shall not cut my thumb.
I've got him!—no, at him again!
  Come, come, I'm not fond of these jokes;
This must be some blade of the brain—
  Those witches are given to hoax.

I've one in my pocket, I know,
  My wife left on purpose behind her;
She bought this of Teddy-high-ho,
  The poor Caledonian grinder.

I see thee again! o'er thy middle
　　Large drops of red blood now are spill'd,
Just as much as to say, diddle diddle,
　　Good Duncan, pray come and be kill'd.

It leads to his chamber, I swear;
　　I tremble and quake every joint—
No dog at the scent of a hare
　　Ever yet made a cleverer point.
Ah, no! 'twas a dagger of straw—
　　Give me blinkers, to save me from starting;
The knife that I thought that I saw
　　Was nought but my eye, Betty Martin.

Now o'er this terrestrial hive
　　A life paralytic is spread;
For while the one half is alive,
　　The other is sleepy and dead.
King Duncan, in grand majesty,
　　Has got my state-bed for a snooze;
I've lent him my slippers, so I
　　May certainly stand in his shoes.

Blow softly, ye murmuring gales!
　　Ye feet, rouse no echo in walking!
For though a dead man tells no tales,
　　Dead walls are much given to talking.
This knife shall be in at the death—
　　I'll stick him, then off safely get!
Cries the world, this could not be Macbeth,
　　For he'd ne'er stick at any thing yet.

Hark, hark! 'tis the signal, by goles!
　　It sounds like a funeral knell;

George Colman the Younger Esqr

MACBETH TRAVESTIE

O, hear it not, Duncan! it tolls
    To call thee to heaven or hell.
Or if you to heaven won't fly,
    But rather prefer Pluto's ether,
Only wait a few years till I die,
    And we'll go to the devil together.
                  Ri fol de rol, &c.

CASE, NO. II

THE STRANGER

W H O has e'er been at Drury must needs know the Stranger,
A wailing old Methodist, gloomy and wan,
A husband suspicious—his wife acted Ranger,
She took to her heels, and left poor Hypocon.
Her martial gallant swore that truth was a libel,
That marriage was thraldom, elopement no sin;
Quoth she, I remember the words of my Bible—
My spouse is a Stranger, and I'll take him in.
   With my sentimentalibus lachrymæ roar'em,
   And pathos and bathos delightful to see;
   And chop and change ribs, à-la-mode Germanorum,
   And high diddle ho diddle, pop tweedle dee.

To keep up her dignity no longer rich enough,
Where was her plate?—why, 'twas laid on the shelf;
Her land fuller's earth, and her great riches kitchen-stuff—
Dressing the dinner instead of herself.
No longer permitted in diamonds to sparkle,
Now plain Mrs. Haller, of servants the dread,
With a heart full of grief, and a pan full of charcoal,
She lighted the company up to their bed.

Incensed at her flight, her poor Hubby in dudgeon
Roam'd after his rib in a gig and a pout,
Till, tired with his journey, the peevish curmudgeon
Sat down and blubber'd just like a church-spout.
One day, on a bench as dejected and sad he laid,
Hearing a squash, he cried, Damn it, what's that?

STRANGER TRAVESTIE

'Twas a child of the count's, in whose service lived
    Adelaide,
Soused in the river, and squall'd like a cat.

Having drawn his young excellence up to the bank, it
Appear'd that himself was all dripping, I swear;
No wonder he soon became dry as a blanket,
Exposed as he was to the count's *son* and *heir*.
Dear sir, quoth the count, in reward of your valour,
To shew that my gratitude is not mere talk,
You shall eat a beefsteak with my cook, Mrs. Haller,
Cut from the rump with her own knife and fork.

Behold, now the count gave the Stranger a dinner,
With gunpowder-tea, which you know brings a ball,
And, thin as he was, that he might not grow thinner,
He made of the Stranger no stranger at all.
At dinner fair Adelaide brought up a chicken—
A bird that she never had met with before;
But, seeing him, scream'd, and was carried off kicking,
And he bang'd his nob 'gainst the opposite door.

To finish my tale without roundaboutation,
Young master and missee besieged their papa;
They sung a quartetto in grand blubberation—
The Stranger cried, Oh! Mrs. Haller cried, Ah!
Though pathos and sentiment largely are dealt in,
I have no good moral to give in exchange;
For though she, as a cook, might be given to melting,
The Stranger's behaviour was certainly strange,
    With his sentimentalibus lachrymæ roar'em,
    And pathos and bathos delightful to see,
    And chop and change ribs, à-la-mode Germanorum,
    And high diddle ho diddle, pop tweedle dee.

CASE, NO. III

GEORGE BARNWELL

G EORGE B ARNWELL stood at the shop-door.
A customer hoping to find, sir;
His apron was hanging before,
But the tail of his coat was behind, sir.
A lady, so painted and smart,
Cried, Sir, I've exhausted my stock o'late;
I've got nothing left but a groat—
Could you give me four penn'orth of chocolate?
    Rum ti, &c.

Her face was rouged up to the eyes,
Which made her look prouder and prouder;
His hair stood on end with surprise,
And hers with pomatum and powder.
The business was soon understood;
The lady, who wish'd to be more rich,
Cries, Sweet sir, my name is Milwood,
And I lodge at the Gunner's in Shoreditch.
    Rum ti, &c.

Now nightly he stole out, good lack!
And into her lodging would pop, sir;
And often forgot to come back,
Leaving master to shut up the shop, sir.
Her beauty his wits did bereave—
Determined to be quite the crack O,

GEORGE BARNWELL TRAVESTIE

He lounged at the Adam and Eve,
And call'd for his gin and tobacco.
    Rum ti, &c.

And now—for the truth must be told,
Though none of a 'prentice should speak ill—
He stole from the till all the gold,
And ate the lump-sugar and treacle.
In vain did his master exclaim,
Dear George, don't engage with that dragon;
She'll lead you to sorrow and shame,
And leave you the devil a rag on
    Your rum ti, &c.

In vain he entreats and implores
The weak and incurable ninny,
So kicks him at last out of doors,
And Georgy soon spends his last guinea.
His uncle, whose generous purse
Had often relieved him, as I know,
Now finding him grow worse and worse,
Refused to come down with the rhino.
    Rum ti, &c.

Cried Milwood, whose cruel heart's core
Was so flinty that nothing could shock it,
If ye mean to come here any more,
Pray come with more cash in your pocket:
Make nunky surrender his dibs,
Rub his pate with a pair of lead towels,
Or stick a knife into his ribs—
I'll warrant he'll then shew some bowels.
    Rum ti, &c.

A pistol he got from his love—
'Twas loaded with powder and bullet;
He trudged off to Camberwell Grove,
But wanted the courage to pull it.
There's nunky as fat as a hog,
While I am as lean as a lizard;
Here's at you, you stingy old dog!—
And he whips a long knife in his gizzard.
     Rum ti, &c.

All you who attend to my song,
A terrible end of the farce shall see,
If you join the inquisitive throng,
That follow'd poor George to the Marshalsea.
If Milwood were here, dash my wigs,
Quoth he, I would pummel and lam her well;
Had I stuck to my pruins and figs,
I ne'er had stuck nunky at Camberwell.
     Rum ti, &c.

Their bodies were never cut down;
For granny relates with amazement,
A witch bore 'em over the town,
And hung them on Thorowgood's casement.
The neighbours, I've heard the folks say,
The miracle noisily brag on;
And the shop is, to this very day,
The sign of the George and the Dragon.
     Rum ti, &c.

PUNCH'S APOTHEOSIS
BY T. H.

> "Rhymes the rudders are of verses,
> With which, like ships, they steer their courses."
> HUDIBRAS.

Scene draws, and discovers PUNCH *on a throne, surrounded by* LEAR, LADY MACBETH, MACBETH, OTHELLO, GEORGE BARNWELL, HAMLET, GHOST, MACHEATH, JULIET, FRIAR, APOTHECARY, ROMEO, *and* FALSTAFF.—PUNCH *descends, and addresses them in the following*

RECITATIVE

As manager of horses Mr. Merryman is,
So I with you am master of the ceremonies—
These grand rejoicings. Let me see, how name ye 'em?—
Oh, in Greek lingo 'tis E-pi-thalamium.
October's tenth it is: toss up each hat to-day,
And celebrate with shouts our opening Saturday!
On this great night 'tis settled by our manager,
That we, to please great Johnny Bull, should plan a jeer,
Dance a bang-up theatrical cotillion,
And put on tuneful Pegasus a pillion;
That every soul, whether or not a cough he has,
May kick like Harlequin, and sing like Orpheus.
So come, ye pupils of Sir John Gallini,
Spin up a tetotum like Angiolini;
That John and Mrs. Bull, from ale and tea-houses,
May shout huzza for Punch's Apotheosis!

REJECTED ADDRESSES

They dance and sing.
Air—" *Sure such a day.*" Tom Thumb.

Lear

Dance, Regan! dance, with Cordelia and Goneril—
Down the middle, up again, poussette, and cross;
Stop, Cordelia! do not tread upon her heel,
Regan feeds on coltsfoot, and kicks like a horse.
See, she twists her mutton fists like Molyneux or Beelzebub,
And t'other's clack, who pats her back, is louder far than hell's hubbub.
They tweak my nose, and round it goes—I fear they'll break the ridge of it,
Or leave it all just like Vauxhall, with only half the bridge of it.

Omnes

Round let us bound, for this is Punch's holyday,
Glory to Tomfoolery, huzza! huzza!

Lady Macbeth

I kill'd the king; my husband is a heavy dunce;
He left the grooms unmassacred, then massacred the stud.
One loves long gloves; for mittens, like king's evidence,
Let truth with the fingers out, and won't hide blood.

Macbeth

When spoonys on two knees implore the aid of sorcery,
To suit their wicked purposes they quickly put the laws awry;
With Adam I in wife may vie, for none could tell the use of her,

Theodore Hook

PUNCH'S APOTHEOSIS

Except to cheapen golden pippins hawk'd about by
    Lucifer.

OMNES

Round let us bound, for this is Punch's holyday,
Glory to Tomfoolery, huzza! huzza!

OTHELLO

Wife, come to life, forgive what your black lover did,
Spit the feathers from your mouth, and munch roast
    beef;
Iago he may go and be toss'd in the coverlid
That smother'd you, because you pawn'd my handkerchief.

GEORGE BARNWELL

Why, neger, so eager about your rib immaculate?
Milwood shews for hanging us they've got an ugly
    knack o' late;
If on beauty 'stead of duty but one peeper bent he sees,
Satan waits with Dolly baits to hook in us apprentices.

OMNES

Round let us bound, for this is Punch's holyday,
Glory to Tomfoolery, huzza! huzza!

HAMLET

I'm Hamlet in camlet, my ap and perihelia
The moon can fix, which lunatics makes sharp or flat.
I stuck by ill luck, enamour'd of Ophelia,
Old Polony like a sausage, and exclaim'd, " Rat, rat! "

GHOST

Let Gertrude sup the poison'd cup—no more I'll be an
    actor in

Such sorry food, but drink home-brew'd of Whitbread's manufacturing.

Macheath
I'll Polly it, and folly it, and dance it quite the dandy O;
But as for tunes, I have but one, and that is Drops of Brandy O.

Omnes
Round let us bound, for this is Punch's holyday,
Glory to Tomfoolery, huzza! huzza!

Juliet
I'm Juliet Capulet, who took a dose of hellebore—
A hell-of-a-bore I found it to put on a pall.

Friar
And I am the friar, who so corpulent a belly bore.

Apothecary
And that is why poor skinny I have none at all.

Romeo
I'm the resurrection-man, of buried bodies amorous.

Falstaff
I'm fagg'd to death, and out of breath, and am for quiet clamorous;
For though my paunch is round and stanch, I ne'er begin to feel it ere I
Feel that I have no stomach left for entertainment military.

PUNCH'S APOTHEOSIS

OMNES

Round let us bound, for this is Punch's holyday,
Glory to Tomfoolery, huzza! huzza!
[*Exeunt dancing.*

THE END

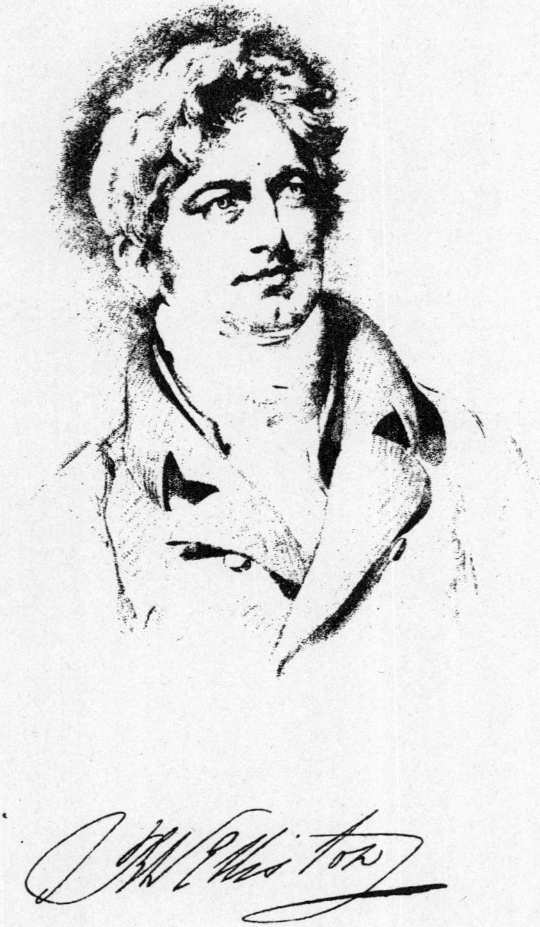

NOTES

I

LOYAL EFFUSION. By W. T. FITZGERALD

WILLIAM THOMAS FITZGERALD (1759-1829), the Laureate of the Literary Fund, was educated at Greenwich and Paris, and studied awhile for the Bar. He drifted into amateur theatricals and from writing prologues came to writing on all sorts of occasions. His verse was much in demand and appreciated by those to whom he gave the rant they wanted. He was one of the founders of the Literary Fund, and always turned up at the dinners with his paper of verses.

James Smith's note is as follows: " The annotator's first personal knowledge of this gentleman was at Harry Greville's Pic-Nic Theatre, in Tottenham-street, where he personated Zanga in a wig too small for his head. The second time of seeing him was at the table of old Lord Dudley, who familiarly called him Fitz, but forgot to name him in his will. The Earl's son (recently deceased), however, liberally supplied the omission by a donation of five thousand pounds. The third and last time of encountering him was at an anniversary dinner of the Literary Fund, at the Freemasons' Tavern. Both parties, as two of the stewards, met their brethren in a small room about half an hour before dinner. The lampooner, out of delicacy, kept aloof from the poet. The latter, however, made up to him, when the following dialogue took place:

NOTES

Fitzgerald (with good humour). ' Mr. ——, I mean to recite after dinner.'

Mr. ——. ' Do you? '

Fitzgerald. ' Yes; you'll have more of " God bless the Regent and the Duke of York!"'

The whole of this imitation [Smith adds], after a lapse of twenty years, appears to the Authors too personal and sarcastic; but they may shelter themselves under a very broad mantle:

  Let [Shall] hoarse Fitzgerald bawl
 His creaking couplets in a tavern-hall. BYRON." J. S.

Byron's note to this was: " Mr. Fitzgerald, facetiously termed by Cobbett the ' Small-Beer Poet,' inflicts his annual tribute of verse on the ' Literary Fund '; not content with writing, he spouts in person, after the company have imbibed a reasonable quantity of bad port, to enable them to sustain the operation."

Later he annotated this: " Right enough: but why notice such a mountebank? "

" Fitzgerald [says James Smith] actually sent in an address to the committee on the 31st of August, 1812. It was published among the other genuine *Rejected Addresses* in one volume, in that year. The following is an extract:—

  The troubled shade of Garrick, hovering near,
  Dropt on the burning pile a pitying tear.

What a pity that, like Sterne's recording angel, it did not succeed in blotting the fire out for ever! That failing, why not adopt Gulliver's remedy? " J. S.

The following is Fitzgerald's Address:—

132

NOTES

Address

Sent to the Committee August 31, 1812
By William Thomas Fitzgerald, Esq.

When wrapped in flames, terrific to the sight,
Old Drury perish'd in one fatal night,
The troubled shade of Garrick, hovering near,
Dropt on the burning pile a pitying tear!
For oft, permitted from the realms above,
Departed spirits watch the place they love.
Rising from ruins, purified by fire,
Behold our renovated Fane aspire
To hold the Drama's mirror to mankind,
Reform the morals and improve the mind.
   In earlier days, offended Wisdom sigh'd
At Wit deprav'd and talents misapplied:
When grossest ribaldry in Charles's reign,
Encouraged Vice, and gave fair Virtue pain:
For brightest Wit became its own disgrace,
That raised a blush on Beauty's modest face!
Licentious Plays debauch'd—the Actors too,
They copied manners which their Authors drew,
Then, like Chameleons, took the tainted hue:
Hence gloomy bigots vilify the Stage,
And hand the libel down from age to age.
   But yet the Drama, rightly understood,
Promotes the private and the public good;
With noblest ardour warms ingenuous youth,
To tread the paths of Virtue, Honour, Truth;
And points where Hist'ry gives to deathless fame,
The Statesman's counsels, and the Hero's name;
Proving, when love of country fades away,
That nations hasten to assur'd decay!
And purer ethics ne'er were taught by Sage

NOTES

Than what abound in Shakespeare's moral page.
That mighty master of the human heart
Bids every Briton act the Patriot's part;
Bids him, obedient to his country's call,
Bear on his shield defiance to the Gaul;
And plum'd in Liberty's immortal crest,
Wage war with Tyrants to relieve th'opprest;
For, still unfetter'd as his native wave,
A Briton's birthright is to scorn a slave!
　Long may the Fabric flourish, and withstand
Devouring flames, and Time's corroding hand!
Here shall be placed and fear no second fire,
The Muse's records and *Apollo's* lyre,
Genius, unaided by a Patron's name,
May here commence his free career of fame;
No favour'd rival shall his course impede,
No envy rob him of the public meed:
But like all vot'ries of the Drama's cause,
Be rul'd like Britons, by impartial Laws.

　The anonymous author of the obituary notice of Horace Smith who wrote this imitation, in the *New Monthly Magazine* (1849), has the following: " Unfortunately several of the characters whose styles were imitated have passed into obscurity and the keenness of the satire cannot now always be understood. The stolidity of Fitzgerald, for example, rendered so much more amusing by his unconsciousness of it, both as to his voice and recitations at the Literary Fund Dinners, cannot be comprehended by the present generation; yet Fitzgerald's was among the most happy of the imitations."

　" The first piece," says the *Edinburgh Review* (1812), " under the name of the loyal Mr. Fitzgerald, though as

134

NOTES

good we suppose as the original, is not very interesting. Whether it be like Mr. Fitzgerald or not [the *Quarterly* also disclaimed to have read Fitzgerald], however, it must be allowed that the vulgarity, servility and gross absurdity of the newspaper scribblers is well rendered in the following lines."

Leigh Hunt wrote: " Mr. Fitzgerald found himself bankrupt in *non sequiturs*."

Fitzgerald seems to have been well liked generally, and was an honest and good-tempered man; but as Canning said at the Literary Fund Dinner, " Poeta nascitur non Fitz."

NOTES

p. 37, *l.* 18. Wyatt, the architect of the theatre, was son of James Wyatt the designer of the Pantheon in Oxford Street, now occupied by Messrs. Gilbey.

p. 38, *l.* 6. Covent Garden Theatre was burnt down Sept. 20, 1808; Drury Lane Theatre Feb. 24, 1809; Astley's in 1794; the Pantheon 1792 and 1803; and the Royal Circus 1805.

p. 38, *l.* 11. In plain English, the Halfpenny-hatch, then a footway through fields, but now, as the same bards sing elsewhere:—

> St. George's Fields are fields no more,
> The trowel supersedes the plough;
> Swamps, huge and inundate of yore,
> Are changed to civic villas now.   J. S.

p. 38, *l.* 23. Luddites were the machine breakers who thought the introduction of machinery would lessen employment. They were so named from Ned Lud, who broke two stocking frames.

p. 38, *l.* 26. The east end of St. James's Palace was burned Jan. 21st, 1809, and the wardrobe of Lady Charlotte Finch was destroyed in it.

p. 38, *l.* 31. The Hon. William Wellesley Pole had carried off Miss Long, the much-sought-after heiress of Sir James Tylney Long, Bart., and assumed on his marriage the names of Tylney and Pole. He became later Earl of Mornington.

NOTES

II

THE BABY'S DEBUT. By WILLIAM WORDSWORTH

WILLIAM WORDSWORTH (1770-1850) had published at the appearance of the *Rejected Addresses* some of his best work. His excursions into the mawkish were singled out here for imitation, and in their 1833 Preface (see p. 24) the brothers Smith make an apology for this in a handsome compliment to the Author. None but a chauvinist admirer of Wordsworth would not smile at this effort of James Smith which is truly in the secondary Wordsworth manner. It is to be regretted that there is on record no expression of Wordsworth's opinion of it. Southey wrote to Sir W. W. Wynn (July 16 1813): " Those [imitations] of Wordsworth and Coleridge appear to me wholly despicable, quite worthy of the mocking bird's original strain." An indication of Wordsworth's feelings may be found in a sympathetic reference of Lamb who, writing to condole with Wordsworth on the spurious Peter Bell (really written by John Hamilton Reynolds), speculates as to the author: " I should guess, one of the sneering brothers, the vile Smiths." Jeffrey, in the *Edinburgh Review* (1812), says:

" The author does not, in this instance, attempt to copy any of the higher attributes of Mr. Wordsworth's poetry; but has succeeded perfectly in the imitation of his mawkish affectations of childish simplicity and nursery stammering. We hope it will make him ashamed of his *Alice Fell*, and the greater part of his last volumes—of which it is by no means a parody, but a very fair, and indeed we think a flattering, imitation."

NOTES

p. 40, *l.* 1. Jack and Nancy, as it was afterwards remarked to the Authors, are here made to come into the world at periods not sufficiently remote. The writers were then bachelors. One of them [James], unfortunately, still continues so, as he has thus recorded in his niece's album:

" Should I seek Hymen's tie,
 As a poet I die—
Ye Benedicks, mourn my distresses!
For what little fame
Is annexed to my name
Is derived from *Rejected Addresses.*"

The blunder, notwithstanding, remains unrectified. The reader of poetry is always dissatisfied with emendations: they sound discordantly upon the ear, like a modern song, by Bishop or Braham, introduced in *Love in a Village.* J. S.

p. 42, *l.* 25. This alludes to the young Betty mania. The writer was in the stage-box at the height of this young gentleman's popularity. One of the other occupants offered, in a loud voice, to prove that young Betty did not understand Shakespeare. " Silence! " was the cry; but he still proceeded. " Turn him out! " was the next ejaculation. He still vociferated " He does not understand Shakespeare; " and was consequently shouldered into the lobby. " I'll prove it to you," said the critic to the door-keeper. " Prove what, sir? " " That he does not understand Shakespeare." This was Molière's housemaid with a vengeance!

Young Betty may now [1833] be seen walking about town —a portly personage, aged about forty—clad in a furred and frogged surtout; probably muttering to himself (as he has been at college), " O mihi præteritos! " &c. J. S. [He died 1874.] Master Betty, or the " Young Roscius," was born in 1791, and made his first appearance on a London stage as Achmet in *Barbarossa*, at Covent Garden Theatre, on the 1st of December, 1804. He was, therefore, " not quite thirteen." P.C. His last appearance was in 1808, after which he went to Christchurch, Cambridge.

NOTES

III

S. T. P., SANCTAE THEOLOGIAE PROFESSOR

THIS, as the 1833 Preface explains (see p. 25), was written seriously by Horace Smith to compete for the Address, before the brothers had decided to write the *Rejected Addresses*. It was added to the book to make bulk, and mystified (as it might well mystify in a book professedly of parodies) the Edinburgh Reviewer. "An address by S. T. P. we can make nothing of; and professing our ignorance of the author designated by these letters we can only add that the Address, though a little affected and not very full of meaning, has no very prominent trait of absurdity that we can detect; and might have been adopted and spoken, so far as we can perceive, without any hazard of ridicule. In our simplicity we consider it as a very decent, mellifluous, occasional prologue and do not understand how it has found its way into its present company." Mr. Percy Fitzgerald speaks of the "unsuspicious gravity of the reviewer—'literal rogue!' Elia would call him." And the brothers speak of their amusement at the mysticism [mystification?], qualified as it was by the poor compliment that our carefully written Address exhibited " no very prominent trait of absurdity." It was surely the Reviewer who scored here; a trap had been set for him, i.e. to treat it as a burlesque and he had not fallen into it.

NOTE

p. 44, Title. A "Phœnix" was perhaps excusable. The first theatre in Drury Lane was called "The Cock-pit or Phœnix Theatre." Whitbread himself wrote an address, it is said, for the occasion; like the others, it had of course a Phœnix. "But Whitbread," said Sheridan, "made more of the bird than any of them; he entered into particulars, and described its wings, beak, tail, &c.; in short, it was a *poulterer's* description of a Phœnix." P. C.

NOTES

IV
CUI BONO? LORD BYRON

LORD BYRON (1788-1824) was one of the earliest and most faithful admirers of the *Rejected Addresses*. On October 19th, while smarting under the criticism of his own Address, he wrote to John Murray: " I think the Rejected Addresses by far the best thing of the kind since the Rolliad and wish *you* had published them. Tell the author I forgive him, were he twenty times over a satirist; and think his imitations not at all inferior to the famous ones of Hawkins Browne. He must be a man of very lively wit, and less scurrilous than wits often are; altogether I very much admire the performance and wish it all success." Again on the 23rd October: " I like the volume of Rejected Addresses better and better." In conversations reported by the Countess of Blessington he always spoke in terms of praise of the *Rejected Addresses*. " Parodies," he said, " give as a rule a bad impression of the originals, but in the ' Rejected Addresses ' the reverse is the fact." Again, in his controversy with Bowles, he illustrates his argument that ridicule does not necessarily imply envy by quoting the case of the *Rejected Addresses*. He confessed to Leigh Hunt that the summing up of his philosophy to wit that " Nought is everything, and everything is nought " was very posing.

Southey wrote: " Of the *Rejected Addresses* I liked Lord Byron best; there were others equally good but here the mode of thought as well as the manner is happily caught." Letter to Sir W. W. Wynn 1813.

Jeffrey wrote in the *Edinburgh Review*: " The author has succeeded better in copying the melody and misanthropic sentiments of *Childe Harold*, than the nervous

NOTES

and impetuous diction in which his noble biographer has embodied them. The attempt, however, indicates very considerable power; and the flow of the verse and the construction of the poetical period are imitated with no ordinary skill."

James Smith's note on Byron in the eighteenth edition is as follows: " This would seem to shew that poet and prophet are synonymous, the noble bard having afterwards returned to England, and again quitted it, under domestic circumstances painfully notorious. His good-humoured forgiveness of the Authors has been already alluded to in the preface. Nothing of this illustrious poet, however trivial, can be otherwise than interesting. 'We knew him well.' At Mr. Murray's dinner-table the annotator met him and Sir John Malcolm. Lord Byron talked of intending to travel in Persia. ' What must I do when I set off? ' said he to Sir John. " Cut off your buttons! ' ' My buttons! what, these metal ones? ' ' Yes; the Persians are in the main very honest fellows; but if you go thus bedizened, you will infallibly be murdered for your buttons! ' At a dinner at Monk Lewis's chambers in the Albany, Lord Byron expressed to the writer his determination not to go there again, adding, ' I never will dine with a middle-aged man who fills up his table with young ensigns, and has looking-glass panels to his book-cases.' Lord Byron, when one of the Drury-lane Committee of Management, challenged the writer to sing alternately (like the swains in Virgil) the praises of Mrs. Mardyn, the actress, who, by the by, was hissed off the stage for an imputed intimacy of which she was quite innocent.

" The contest ran as follows:
  ' Wake, muse of fire, your ardent lyre,
   Pour forth your amorous ditty,

NOTES

> But first profound, in duty bound,
>   Applaud the new committee;
> Their scenic art from Thespis' cart
>   All jaded nags discarding,
> To London drove this queen of love,
>   Enchanting Mrs. Mardyn.
>
> Though tides of love around her rove,
>   I fear she'll choose Pactolus—
> In that bright surge bards ne'er immerge,
>   So I must e'en swim solus.
> " Out, out, alas! " ill-fated gas,
>   That shin'st round Covent Garden,
> Thy ray how flat, compared with that
>   From eye of Mrs. Mardyn! '

And so on. The reader has, no doubt, already discovered ' which is the justice, and which is the thief.'

" Lord Byron at that time wore a very narrow cravat of white sarsnet, with the shirt-collar falling over it; a black coat and waistcoat, and very broad white trousers, to hide his lame foot—these were of Russia duck in the morning, and jean in the evening. His watch-chain had a number of small gold seals appended to it, and was looped up to a button of his waistcoat. His face was void of colour; he wore no whiskers. His eyes were grey, fringed with long black lashes; and his air was imposing, but rather supercilious. He undervalued David Hume; denying his claim to genius on account of his bulk, and calling him, from the Heroic Epistle,

> ' The fattest hog in Epicurus' sty.'

One of this extraordinary man's allegations was, that ' fat is an oily dropsy.' To stave off its visitation, he

NOTES

frequently chewed tobacco in lieu of dinner, alleging that it absorbed the gastric juice of the stomach, and prevented hunger. ' Pass your hand down my side,' said his Lordship to the writer; ' can you count my ribs? ' ' Every one of them.' ' I am delighted to hear you say so. I called last week on Lady ——; "Ah, Lord Byron," said she, " how fat you grow! " But you know Lady —— is fond of saying spiteful things! ' Let this gossip be summed up with the words of Lord Chesterfield, in his character of Bolingbroke: ' Upon the whole, on a survey of this extraordinary character, what can we say, but "Alas, poor human nature! " '

" His favourite Pope's description of man is applicable to Byron individually:

' Chaos of thought and passion all confused,
Still by himself abused or disabused;
Created part to rise and part to fall,
Great lord of all things, yet a slave to all;
Sole judge of truth, in endless error hurled—
The glory, jest, and riddle of the world.'

" The writer never heard him allude to his deformed foot except upon one occasion, when, entering the green-room of Drury-lane, he found Lord Byron alone, the younger Byrne and Miss Smith the dancer having just left him, after an angry conference about a *pas seul*. ' Had you been here a minute sooner,' said Lord B., ' you would have heard a question about dancing referred to me;—me! (looking mournfully downward) whom'fate from my birth has prohibited from taking a single step.' " J. S.

The first stanza was written by James—the rest by Horace—and must rank as one of the best things he ever did.

NOTES

p. 47, *l.* 27. "Holland's edifice." The late theatre was built by Holland the architect. The writer visited it on the night of its opening [April 21, 1794]. The performances were *Macbeth* and the *Virgin Unmasked*. Between the play and the farce, an excellent epilogue, written by George Colman, was excellently spoken by Miss Farren. It referred to the iron curtain which was, in the event of fire, to be let down between the stage and the audience, and which accordingly descended, by way of experiment, leaving Miss Farren between the lamps and the curtain. The fair speaker informed the audience that should the fire break out on the stage (where it usually originates), it would thus be kept from the spectators; adding, with great solemnity—

"No! we assure our generous benefactors
'Twill only burn the scenery and the actors!"

A tank of water was afterwards exhibited, in the course of the epilogue, in which a wherry was rowed by a real live man, the band playing—

"And did you not hear of a jolly young waterman?"

Miss Farren reciting—

"Sit still, there's nothing in it,
We'll undertake to drown you in a single minute."

"O vain thought!" as Othello says. Notwithstanding the boast in the epilogue—

"Blow, wind—come, rack, in ages yet unborn,
Our castle's strength shall laugh a siege to scorn"—

the theatre fell a victim to the flames within fifteen years from the prognostic! These preparations against fire always presuppose presence of mind and promptness in those who are to put them into action. They remind one of the dialogue, in Morton's *Speed the Plough*, between Sir Able Handy and his son Bob:

"*Bob.* Zounds, the castle's on fire!
Sir A. Yes.
Bob. Where's your patent liquid for extinguishing fire?
Sir A. It is not mixed.
Bob. Then where's your patent fire-escape?

NOTES

Sir A. It is not fixed.
Bob. You are never at a loss?
Sir A. Never.
Bob. Then what do you mean to do?
Sir A. I don't know." J. S.

p. 48, *l.* 25. A rather obscure mode of expression for Jew's-harp which some etymologists allege, by the way, to be a corruption of Jaw's-harp. No connexion, therefore, with King David. J. S.

Here follows Byron's accepted Address; its history and criticism are dealt with in the Preface. See p. 2 *et seq.*

ADDRESS, SPOKEN at the OPENING of DRURY-LANE THEATRE
Saturday October 10th 1812

In one dread night our city saw, and sigh'd,
Bow'd to the dust, the Drama's tower of pride;
In one short hour before the blazing fane,
Apollo sink and Shakspeare cease to reign.
 Ye who beheld, (oh! sight admired and mourn'd,
Whose radiance mock'd the ruin it adorn'd!)
Through clouds of fire the massy fragments riven,
Like Israel's pillar, chase the night from heaven;
Saw the long column of revolving flames
Shake its red shadow o'er the startled Thames,
While thousands throng'd around the burning dome,
Shrank back appall'd, and trembled for their home,
As glared the volumed blaze and ghastly shone
The skies with lightnings awful as their own,
Till blackened ashes and the lonely wall
Usurp'd the Muse's realm and mark'd her fall;
Say, shall this new, nor less aspiring pile,
Rear'd where once rose the mightiest in our isle,
Know the same favour which the former knew,

NOTES

A shrine for Shakspeare—worthy him and *you*?
Yes—it shall be—the magic of that name
Defies the scythe of time, the torch of flame;
On the same spot still consecrates the scene,
And bids the Drama *be* where she hath *been;*
This fabric's birth attests the potent spell
Indulge our honest pride, and say, *How well!*

   As soars this fane to emulate the last,
Oh! might we draw our omens from the past,
Some hour propitious to our prayers may boast
Names such as hallow still the dome we lost.
On Drury first your Siddons' thrilling art
O'erwhelm'd the gentlest, storm'd the sternest heart.
On Drury, Garrick's latest laurels grew;
Here your last tears retiring Roscius drew,
Sigh'd his last thanks, and wept his last adieu:
But still for living wit the wreaths may bloom,
That only waste their odours o'er the tomb.
Such Drury claim'd and claims—nor you refuse
One tribute to revive his slumbering muse;
With garlands deck your own Menander's head,
Nor hoard your honours idly for the dead.
Dear are the days which made our annals bright,
Ere Garrick fled, or Brinsley ceased to write.
Heirs to their labours, like all high-born heirs,
Vain of *our* ancestry as they of *theirs;*
While thus Remembrance borrows Banquo's glass
To claim the sceptred shadows as they pass,
And we the mirror hold, where imaged shine
Immortal names, emblazon'd on our line,
Pause—ere their feebler offspring you condemn,
Reflect how hard the task to rival them!

   Friends of the stage! to whom both Players and Plays
Must sue alike for pardon or for praise,

NOTES

Whose judging voice and eye alone direct
The boundless power to cherish or reject;
If e'er frivolity has led to fame,
And made us blush that you forbore to blame;
If e'er the sinking stage could condescend
To soothe the sickly taste it dare not mend,
All past reproach may present scenes refute,
And censure, wisely loud, be justly mute!
Oh! since your fiat stamps the Drama's laws,
Forbear to mock us with misplaced applause;
So pride shall doubly nerve the actor's powers,
And reason's voice be echo'd back by ours!
   This greeting o'er, the ancient rule obey'd
The Drama's homage by her herald paid,
Receive our welcome too, whose every tone
Springs from our hearts, and fain would win your own.
The curtain rises—may our stage unfold
Scenes not unworthy Drury's days of old!
Britons our judges, Nature for our guide,
Still may we please—long, long may you preside.

V

HAMPSHIRE FARMER'S ADDRESS
By WILLIAM COBBETT

WILLIAM COBBETT (1762-1835), was the greatest English Radical. He never supported an opinion which he did not live to attack nor praised a man whom he did not live to censure. The imitation Address was written by James Smith in the style of his *Weekly Register*, and is admirable in all respects. Unfortunately we have not Cobbett's opinion on it, nor yet any contemporary one.

NOTES

p. 51, *l.* 15. The Weekly Register, which he kept up without the failure of a single week, from its first publication till his death—a period of above thirty-three years. P. C.

p. 52, *l.* 18. Bagshaw. At that time the publisher of Cobbett's Register. J. S.

p. 52, *l.* 18. The old Lyceum Theatre, pulled down by Mr. Arnold. That since destroyed by fire [16 Feb., 1830] was erected on its site. J. S. It was here that the Drury Lane Company performed during the rebuilding of their own theatre.

p. 53, *l.* 22. O. P. See post p.149.

p. 53, *l.* 34. The present colonnades were subsequently built.

p. 54, *l.* 18. An allusion to a murder then recently committed on Barnes Terrace. J. S. The murder (22nd July, 1812) of the Count and Countess D'Antraigues (distantly related to the Bourbons), by a servant out of livery of the name of Laurence—an Italian or Piedmontese, who made away with himself immediately after. P. C.

p. 55, *l.* 12. At that time keeper of Newgate. The present superintendent (1833) is styled Governor! J. S.

p. 55, *l.* 16. A portentous one that made its appearance in the year 1811; in the midst of the war,

" with fear of change
Perplexing nations." J. S.

VI

THE LIVING LUSTRES. By THOMAS MOORE

THOMAS MOORE (1780-1852), the Irish Patriot and Love Poet whose practice of drifting from one to the other—both apropos of something else—is admirably touched off in this imitation by Horace Smith. Moore knew both the Smiths and has left records of them,

NOTES

although James in his notes makes no mention of Moore. See post in note on Crabbe.

Jeffrey, in the *Edinburgh Review*, says: " *The Living Lustres* appears to us a very fair imitation of the fantastic verses which that ingenious person, Mr. Moore, indites when he is merely gallant, and, resisting the lures of voluptuousness, is not enough in earnest to be tender."

NOTES

p. 57, *l.* 11. This alludes to two massive pillars of verd antique which then flanked the proscenium, but which have since been removed. Their colour reminds the bard of the Emerald Isle, and this causes him (*more suo*) to fly off at a tangent, and Hibernicise the rest of the poem. J. S.

p. 58, *l.* 7. Sir Vicary Gibbs and Sir William Garrow were the Attorneys-General at the time. Leigh Hunt, speaking of his own trial: " Mr. Garrow, the Attorney-General, (who had succeeded Sir Vicary Gibbs at a very cruel moment, for the indictment had been brought by that irritable person and was the first against us which took effect) behaved to us with a politeness that was considered extraordinary."

VII
THE REBUILDING. By ROBERT SOUTHEY

ROBERT SOUTHEY (1774-1843), Poet Laureate. When the *Rejected Addresses* appeared, Southey had completely turned his back on his former radical principles and was next year to receive as a reward the Laureateship which Sir Walter Scott, who refused it, secured for him. This imitation by James Smith is excellent. Southey wrote: " That of ' Kehama ' is not so good because it is not so close." Letter to Sir W. W. Wynn. A contemporary, Ward, afterwards Lord Dudley and

NOTES

Ward, in a letter to Mrs. Dugald Stewart, considered it the best.

Jeffrey, in the *Edinburgh Review*, says: " *The Rebuilding* is in the name of Mr. Southey, and is one of the best in the collection. It is in the style of the Kehama of that multifarious author, and is supposed to be spoken in the character of one of his Glendoveers. The imitation of the diction and measure, we think, is nearly almost perfect; and the descriptions as good as the original. It opens with an account of the burning of the old theatre, formed upon the pattern of the Funeral of Arvalan."

NOTES

p. 59, *l.* 1. For the Glendoveer, and the rest of the *dramatis personæ* of this imitation, the reader is referred to the " Curse of Kehama."   J. S.

p. 59, *l.* 18. This couplet was introduced by the Authors by way of bravado, in answer to one who alleged that the English language contained no rhyme to chimney.   J. S.

p. 60, *l.* 4. Apollo. A gigantic wooden figure of this deity was erected on the roof. The writer (*horrescit referens!*) is old enough to recollect the time when it was first placed there. Old Bishop, then one of the masters of Merchant Tailors' School, wrote an epigram upon the occasion, which, referring to the aforesaid figure, concluded thus:

" Above he fills up Shakespeare's place,
And Shakespeare fills up his below."

Very antithetical; but quære as to the meaning? The writer, like Pluto, " long puzzled his brain " to find it out, till he was immersed " in a lower deep " by hearing Madame de Staël say, at the table of the late Lord Dillon, " Buonaparte is not a man, but a system." Inquiry was made in the course of the evening of Sir James Mackintosh as to what the lady meant? He answered, " Mass! I cannot tell." Madame de Staël repeats this apophthegm in her work on Germany. It is probably understood *there*.   J. S.

p. 61, *l.* 19. O. P. This personage, who is alleged to have

NOTES

growled like a bull-dog, requires rather a lengthened note, for the edification of the rising generation. The " horns, rattles, drums," with which he is accompanied, are no inventions of the poet. The new Covent Garden Theatre opened on the 18th Sept., 1809, when a cry of " Old Prices " (afterwards diminished to O. P.) burst out from every part of the house. This continued and increased in violence till the 23rd, when rattles, drums, whistles, and cat-calls having completely drowned the voices of the actors, Mr. Kemble, the stage-manager, came forward and said that a committee of gentlemen had undertaken to examine the finances of the concern, and that until they were prepared with their report the theatre would continue closed. " Name them! " was shouted from all sides. The names were declared, viz., Sir Charles Price, the Solicitor-General, the Recorder of London, the Governor of the Bank, and Mr. Angerstein. " All shareholders! " bawled a wag from the gallery. In a few days the theatre re-opened: the public paid no attention to the report of the referees, and the tumult was renewed for several weeks with even increased violence. The proprietors now sent in hired bruisers, to *mill* the refractory into subjection. This irritated most of their former friends, and, amongst the rest, the annotator, who accordingly wrote the song of " Heigh-ho, says Kemble," which was caught up by the ballad-singers, and sung under Mr. Kemble's house-windows in Great Russell-street. A dinner was given at the Crown and Anchor Tavern in the Strand, to celebrate the victory obtained by W. Clifford in his action against Brandon the box-keeper, for assaulting him for wearing the letters O. P. in his hat. At this dinner Mr. Kemble attended, and matters were compromised by allowing the advanced price (seven shillings) to the boxes. The writer remembers a former riot of a similar sort at the same theatre (in the year 1792), when the price to the boxes was raised from five shillings to six. That tumult, however, only lasted three nights.   J. S.

p. 61, *l.* 32. " From the knobb'd bludgeon to the taper switch." This image is not the creation of the poets: it sprang from reality. The Authors happened to be at the Royal Circus when " God save the King " was called for, accompanied by a cry of " Stand up! " and " Hats off! "

NOTES

An inebriated naval lieutenant, perceiving a gentleman in an adjoining box slow to obey the call, struck his hat off with his stick, exclaiming, " Take off your hat, sir! " The other thus assaulted proved to be, unluckily for the lieutenant, Lord Camelford, the celebrated bruiser and duellist. A set-to in the lobby was the consequence, where his lordship quickly proved victorious. " The devil is not so black as he is painted," said one of the Authors to the other; " let us call upon Lord Camelford, and tell him that we were witnesses of his being first assaulted." The visit was paid on the ensuing morning at Lord Camelford's lodgings, in Bond-street. Over the fire-place in the drawing-room were ornaments strongly expressive of the pugnacity of the peer. A long thick bludgeon lay horizontally supported by two brass hooks. Above this was placed parallel one of lesser dimensions, until a pyramid of weapons gradually arose, tapering to a horsewhip:

" Thus all below was strength, and all above was grace."

Lord Camelford received his visitants with great civility, and thanked them warmly for the call; adding, that their evidence would be material, it being his intention to indict the lieutenant for an assault. " All I can say in return is this," exclaimed the peer with great cordiality, " if ever I see you engaged in a row, upon my soul I'll stand by you." The Authors expressed themselves thankful for so potent an ally, and departed. In about a fortnight afterwards [March 7, 1804] Lord Camelford was shot in a duel with Mr. Best. J. S.

p. 62, *l.* 29. Veeshnoo. The late Mr. Whitbread. J. S.

p. 64, *l.* 33. Levy. An insolvent Israelite who [18th January, 1810] threw himself from the top of the Monument a short time before. An inhabitant of Monument-yard informed the writer that he happened to be standing at his door talking to a neighbour, and looking up at the top of the pillar, exclaimed, " Why, here's the flag coming down." " Flag! " answered the other, " it's a man." The words were hardly uttered when the suicide fell within ten feet of the speakers. J. S.

NOTES

VIII
DRURY'S DIRGE. By LAURA MATILDA

THE Smiths, from their note (below), seemed anxious to disavow any revelation of identity of this author. The truth is a school was meant—the descendants of the Della Cruscans whose mellifluous and harmless verses were demolished by Gifford in his *Baviad*. The name was composite from Laura Maria—Mrs. Robinson (Perdita) and Anna Matilda (Mrs. Hannah Cowley). They were both dead, but their school still flourished in the Poets' Corner of newspapers and miscellanies.

The following is James Smith's note:—"The Authors, as in gallantry bound, wish this lady to continue anonymous. If Mr. Cruickshank intends any ' scandal about Queen Elizabeth,' they beg to disavow any share in the responsibility."

Jeffrey, in the *Edinburgh Review*, writes: " ' Drury's Dirge,' by Laura Matilda, is not of the first quality. The verses, to be sure, are very smooth, and very nonsensical—as was intended; but they are not so good as Swift's celebrated Song by a Person of Quality; and are so exactly in the same measure, and on the same plan, that it is impossible to avoid making the comparison."

IX
A TALE OF DRURY LANE. By WALTER SCOTT

SIR WALTER SCOTT (1771-1832) was, like Byron, a fervid admirer of the *Rejected Addresses*, and became well acquainted with the Authors. As he told James Smith, he felt he must have written the verses himself, and as

NOTES

an instance of catching his spirit, he stated that he had once chosen the same motto for a collection of his works. A letter of his at the time of the publication of the Addresses throws some light on the attitude and feelings of authors towards their imitators. He writes: to Lady Abercorn (23 Mar., 1813) " I am very well diverted indeed with the 'Rejected Addresses' but I really did not think it necessary to express my satisfaction to the Messrs. Smith, the authors. I would certainly have done so had I had a handsome opportunity, but the gentlemen are perfect strangers to me and to intrude a compliment upon them might have looked like deprecating their satire—a point in which my feelings are invulnerable."

Jeffrey, in the *Edinburgh Review*, writes: " ' A Tale of Drury,' by Walter Scott, is, upon the whole, admirably executed; though the introduction is rather tame. The burning is described with the mighty minstrel's characteristic love of localities. . . . The catastrophe is described with a spirit not unworthy of the name so venturously assumed by the describer."

Gifford, in the *Quarterly Review*, says: " From the parody of Walter Scott we know not what to select— it is all good. The effect of the fire on the town, and the description of a fireman in his official apparel, may be quoted as amusing specimens of the *misapplication* of the style and metre of Mr. Scott's admirable romances."

NOTES

p. 70, Motto. Sir Walter Scott informed the annotator, that at one time he intended to print his collected works, and had pitched upon this identical quotation as a motto; —a proof that sometimes great wits jump with little ones. J. S.

NOTES

p. 70, *l.* 13. Alluding to the then great distance between the picture-frame, in which the green curtain was set, and the band. For a justification of this, see below—"DR. JOHNSON." J. S. This was changed later at great expense by Mr. Elliston.

p. 70, *l.* 16. The old name for London:

For poets you can never want 'em
Spread through Augusta Trinobantum.—SWIFT.

Thomson in his " Seasons " calls it " huge Augusta." P.C.

p. 72, *l.* 12. Old Bedlam, at that time, stood " close by London Wall." It was built after the model of the Tuileries, which is said to have given the French king great offence. In front of it Moorfields extended, with broad gravel walks crossing each other at right angles. These the writer well recollects; and Rivaz, an underwriter at Lloyd's, has told him that he remembered when the merchants of London would parade these walks on a summer evening with their wives and daughters. But now, as a punning brother bard sings,

" Moorfields are fields no more." J. S.

p. 73, *l.* 11. A narrow passage immediately adjoining Drury Lane Theatre, and so called from the vineyard attached to Covent or Convent Garden. P. C.

p. 73, *l.* 19. The Hand-in-Hand Insurance Office was one of the very first insurance offices established in London. To make the engineer of the office thus early in the race is a piece of historical accuracy intended, it is said, on the part of the writer. P. C. It was introduced in the Second Edition, the First reading differently. See p. 179. No doubt their city acquaintances pointed this out to the Smiths.

p. 77, *l.* 10. Whitbread's shears. An economical experiment of that gentleman. The present portico, towards Brydges-street, was afterwards erected under the lesseeship of Elliston, whose portrait in the Exhibition was thus noticed in the Examiner: " Portrait of the great Lessee, in his favourite character of Mr. Elliston." J. S.

NOTES

X
JOHNSON'S GHOST

It is not clear why Johnson should have been introduced among living authors. Perhaps in view of his connection with Drury Lane, but more probably because parodies of Johnson were common then, and the brothers felt they could do one easily. It is not of the best, but has been unduly underrated on account of the burlesque in a few phrases. Take the first three paragraphs, omit the fourth, fifth and sixth, and the remainder is excellent and quite in the Johnson manner.

Jeffrey, in the *Edinburgh Review*, writes: " Samuel Johnson is not so good: the measure and solemnity of his sentences, in all the limited variety of their structure, are indeed imitated with singular skill; but the diction is caricatured in a vulgar and unpleasing degree. To make Johnson call a door ' a ligneous barricado,' and its knocker and bell its ' frappant and tintinnabulant appendages,' is neither just nor humorous; and we are surprised that a writer who has given such extraordinary proofs of his talent for finer ridicule and fairer imitation, should have stooped to a vein of pleasantry so low, and so long ago exhausted; especially as, in other passages of the same piece, he has shown how well qualified he was both to catch and to render the true characteristics of his original. The beginning, for example, we think excellent."

NOTES

p. 80, *l*. 32. The celebrated Lord Chesterfield, whose Letters to his Son, according to Dr. Johnson, inculcate " the manners of a dancing-master and the morals of a ——," &c. J. S.

p. 81, *l*. 20. Lord Mayor of the theatric sky. This alludes to Leigh Hunt, who, in *The Examiner*, at this time kept the

NOTES

actors in hot water. Dr. Johnson's argument is, like many of his other arguments, specious, but untenable; that which it defends has since been abandoned as impracticable. Mr. Whitbread contended that the actor was like a portrait in a picture, and accordingly placed the green curtain in a gilded frame remote from the foot-lights; alleging that no performer should mar the illusion by stepping out of the frame. Dowton was the first actor who, like Manfred's ancestor in the *Castle of Otranto*, took the liberty of abandoning the canon. " Don't tell me of frames and pictures," ejaculated the testy comedian; " if I can't be heard by the audience in the frame, I'll walk out of it! " The proscenium has since been new-modelled, and the actors thereby brought nearer to the audience. J. S.

XI

THE BEAUTIFUL INCENDIARY. By the Hon. W. SPENSER

THE HON. W. R. SPENCER (1769-1834) was a popular writer of *vers de société*, and at the time of the publication of the *Rejected Addresses* would be well known to all general readers. Lamb uses his name in an Essay on the " Ambiguities arising from Proper Names," to illustrate the confusion caused by one speaking of Spenser, meaning the Elizabethan, and his companion, thinking of the Hon. W. R. Spencer. The anecdote illustrates at least the fact that Spencer was read a good deal at the time.

James Smith, in his note, says: " The good-humour of the poet upon occasion of this parody has been noticed in the Preface [see p. 29]. ' It's all very well for once,' said he afterwards, in comic confidence, at his villa at Petersham, ' but don't do it again. I had been

NOTES

almost forgotten when you revived me; and now all the newspapers and reviews ring with " this fashionable, trashy author." ' The sand and ' filings of glass,' mentioned in the last stanza, are referable to the well-known verses of the poet apologising to a lady for having paid an unconscionably long morning visit; and where, alluding to Time, he says—

' All his sands are diamond sparks,
That glitter as they pass.'

" Few men in society have more ' gladdened life ' than this poet. He now [1833] resides in Paris, and may thence make the grand tour without an interpreter—speaking, as he does, French, Italian, and German, as fluently as English." J. S.

Jeffrey thus notices this imitation in the *Edinburgh Review*: " ' The Beautiful Incendiary,' by the Honourable W. Spencer, is also an imitation of great merit. The flashy, fashionable, artificial style of this writer, with his confident and extravagant compliments, can scarcely be said to be parodied in such lines."

NOTES

p. 86, *l*. 2. Congreve's plug. The late Sir William Congreve had made a model of Drury Lane Theatre, to which was affixed an engine that, in event of fire, was made to play from the stage into every box in the house. The writer, accompanied by Theodore Hook, went to see the model at Sir William's house in Cecil-street. " Now I'll duck Whitbread! " said Hook, seizing the water-pipe whilst he spoke, and sending a torrent of water into the brewer's box. J. S.

p. 86, *l*. 25. See Byron, *afterwards*, in *Don Juan*:—

" For flesh is grass, which Time mows down to hay."

But as Johnson says of Dryden, " His known wealth was so great, he might borrow without any impeachment of his credit."   J. S.

NOTES
XII
FIRE AND ALE. By MATTHEW GREGORY LEWIS

MATTHEW GREGORY LEWIS (1776-1818) was one of the first of the jocular gothics. Horace Smith has hit him off admirably in this imitation.

James Smith gives the following rather acidulated account of Lewis: " Matthew Gregory Lewis, commonly called *Monk* Lewis, from his once popular romance of that name, was a good-hearted man, and, like too many of that fraternity, a disagreeable one—verbose, disputatious, and paradoxical. His *Monk* and *Castle Spectre* elevated him into fame; and he continued to write ghost stories till, following as he did in the wake of Mrs. Radcliffe, he quite overstocked the market. Lewis visited his estates in Jamaica, and came back perfectly negro-bitten. He promulgated a new code of laws in the island, for the government of his sable subjects: one may serve for a specimen. ' Any slave who commits murder shall have his head shaved, and be confined three days and nights in a dark room.' Upon occasion of printing these parodies, *Monk* Lewis said to Lady H[olland], ' Many of them are very fair, but mine is not at all like; they have made me write burlesque, which I never do.' ' You don't know your own talent,' answered the lady.

" Lewis aptly described himself, as to externals, in the verses affixed to his *Monk*, as having

' A graceless form and dwarfish stature.'

He had, moreover, large grey eyes, thick features, and an inexpressive countenance. In talking, he had a disagreeable habit of drawing the fore-finger of his right hand across his right eye-lid. He affected, in conversation, a sort of dandified, drawling tone: young Harlowe, the artist, did the same. A foreigner who had but a slight knowledge of the English language might have concluded, from their cadences, that they were little better than fools—'just a born goose,' as Terry the actor used to say. Lewis died on his passage homeward from Jamaica, owing to a dose of James's powders injudiciously administered by 'his own mere motion.' He wrote various plays, with various success: he had admirable notions of dramatic construction, but the goodness of his scenes and incidents was marred by the badness of his dialogue." J. S.

Jeffrey thus refers to the imitation in the *Edinburgh Review*; "' Fire and Ale,' by M. G. Lewis, exhibits not only a faithful copy of the spirited, loose, and flowing versification of that singular author, but a very just representation of that mixture of extravagance and jocularity which has impressed most of his writings with the character of a sort of farcical horror."

XIII

PLAYHOUSE MUSINGS. By SAMUEL TAYLOR COLERIDGE

SAMUEL TAYLOR COLERIDGE (1772-1834) had already published most of his best work when the *Rejected Addresses* appeared. James Smith seems at first sight to have selected a very unfamiliar style of Coleridge's to imitate; he chose the most vulnerable side, and in the Preface of the 1833 edition (see p. 24) made amends to

NOTES

him as to Wordsworth. Coleridge does not seem to have relished the parody, for this truly was a parody.

Gifford had written in the *Quarterly Review:* "Mr. Coleridge will not, we fear, be as much entertained as we were with his 'Playhouse Musings,' which begin with characteristic pathos and simplicity, and put us much in mind of the affecting story of old Poulter's mare."

Writing to Southey (Feb. 8, 1813), Coleridge says: " That paragraph in the Quarterly Review respecting me as ridiculed in the *Rejected Addresses* was surely unworthy of a man of sense like Gifford. What reason could he have to suppose me a man so childishly irritable as to be provoked by a trifle so contemptible. If he had, how could he think it a parody at all. But the noise which the *Rejected Addresses* made, the notice taken of Smith the author by Lord Holland, Byron, etc., gives a melancholy confirmation of my assertion in ' The Friend ' that we worship the vilest reptile if only the brainless head be expiated by the sting of personal malignity in the tail."

Southey wrote: " Those of Wordsworth and Coleridge appear to me utterly despicable, quite worthy of the mocking birds original strains." Letter to Sir W. W. Wynn. July 16 1813.

Jeffrey writes in the *Edinburgh Review*: " 'Playhouse Musings,' by Mr. Coleridge, a piece which is unquestionably Lakish, though we cannot say that we recognise in it any of the peculiar traits of that powerful and misdirected genius whose name it has borrowed. We rather think, however, that the tuneful brotherhood will consider it as a respectable eclogue."

NOTES

p. 90, *l.* 18. " He of Blackfriars' Road," viz. the late Rev. Rowland Hill, who is said to have preached a sermon congratulating his congregation on the catastrophe. J. S.

This is Theodore Hook's account: " It may not be amiss to state that at that stye of mud and corruption, Rowland Hill's chapel, the congregation were congratulated from the pulpit on the destruction of Covent Garden Theatre, and the annihilation of a score of firemen, noticed as a singular proof of the wisdom of Providence in these words: ' Great news, my brethren, great news! a great triumph has taken place over the devil and the stage players—a fire in one of their houses. Oh may there be one consumed every year! It is my fervent prayer!' " Preface to " Killing no Murder."

p. 92, *l.* 1. " Oh, Mr. Whitbread! " Sir William Grant, then Master of the Rolls, repeated this passage aloud at a Lord Mayor's dinner, to the no small astonishment of the writer, who happened to sit within ear-shot. J. S.

p. 92, *l.* 28. " Padmanaba," viz., in a pantomime called *Harlequin in Padmanaba*. This elephant [Chunee], some years afterwards, was exhibited over Exeter 'Change, where, the reader will remember, it was found necessary [March, 1826] to destroy the poor animal by discharges of musketry. When he made his entrance in the pantomime above mentioned, Johnson, the machinist of the rival house, exclaimed, " I should be very sorry if I could not make a better elephant than that! " Johnson was right: we go to the theatre to be pleased with the skill of the imitator, and not to look at the reality. J. S.

XIV

DRURY LANE HUSTING

This is a song in the style of the old music-hall artist now almost obsolete. It lasted almost unchanged in style until the end of the nineteenth century. Mr. Percy

NOTES

Fitzgerald says in his notes: " These things were specially written for ' Irish ' Johnstone, one of the many Englishmen who excelled in Irish characters. It is curious to reflect that the present day ' topical song ' of the music halls differs but little from this shape of buffoonery " (1890).

Jeffrey thus stigmatises it in the *Edinburgh Review*: " ' A New Halfpenny Ballad,' by a Pic-Nic Poet, is a good imitation of what was not worth imitating—that tremendous mixture of vulgarity, nonsense, impudence, and miserable puns, which, under the name of humorous songs, rouses our polite audiences to a far higher pitch of rapture than Garrick or Siddons ever was able to inspire."

NOTE

p. 96, *l.* 8. Mr. Whitbread—it need hardly be added for the present generation of Londoners—was a celebrated brewer. Fifty years hence, and the allusion in the text may require a note which, perhaps, even now (1854), is scarcely out of place.   P. C.

XV

ARCHITECTURAL ATOMS. By Dr. THOMAS BUSBY (*Mus. Doc.*)

THOMAS BUSBY (Mus. Doc.) was born 1755, the son of a coach builder at Westminster. His voice attracted attention—he was made a chorister at Westminster Abbey, and was educated at the school. Apprenticed to a music master, he wrote several musical works and a poem—the *Age of Genius*—which was praised by Sir Joshua Reynolds. He was organist at two London churches, and received in 1800 his musical degree from

NOTES

Cambridge University. Some of his operas were quite successful. He wrote the music to Holcroft's *Tale of Mystery*. When Sir Richard Phillips founded the *Monthly Magazine* Busby was one of the first contributors and remained associated with him during his whole career. He wrote for Phillips a musical dictionary which went through many editions, and it is in Phillips's *Public Characters* (1804) that we get the only published portrait of Busby. He seems to have pestered everyone to subscribe to his *Lucretius*, and with some success, for the book was published in two vols., royal 4to, 1813, with a formidable list of subscribers—including Lord Byron, who is referred to as one of the greatest living poets. Twelve years later Busby figures again as the little old man sitting in a kind of wooden pavilion, composing tunes on the pianoforte, when Sir Richard Phillips brings Borrow to him as the future Editor of the *Oxford* [Universal] *Review*. The pile of books, " a translation of Quintilian," of which Borrow refused a copy at a reduced price—was the remainder of Busby's *Lucretius*. He died in 1838.

The following is Dr. Busby's address which his son failed to recite. (See *ante* p. 7).

Monologue

By Dr. Busby

When energizing objects men pursue,
What are the prodigies they cannot do?
A magic Edifice you here survey,
Shot from the ruins of the other day!
As Harlequin had smote the slumberous heap,
And bade the rubbish to a fabric leap.
Yet at the speed you'd never be amazed,

NOTES

Knew you the zeal with which the pile was rais'd:
Nor ever here your smiles would be represt,
Knew you the rival flame that fires our breast.
Flame! fire and flame! sad, heart apalling sounds,
Dread metaphors, that ope our healing wounds—
A sleeping pang awake—and— But away
With all reflections that would cloud the day
That this triumphant, brilliant prospect brings;
Where hope reviving, re-expands her wings:
Where generous joy exults—where duteous ardour
    springs.
  Oft on these boards we've proved— No, not these
    boards—
Th'exalting sanction your applause affords;
Warm'd with the fond remembrance, every nerve
We'll strain, the future honour to deserve:
Give the great work our earnest, strenuous hand,
And (since new tenements new brooms demand)
Rich novelty explore: all merit prize,
And court the living talents as they rise:
Th'illustrious dead revere—yet hope to shew,
The modern bards with ancient genius glow.
Sense we'll consult e'en in our farce and fun,
And without *steeds* our patent stage shall run;
Self-actuated whirl—nor you deny,
While you're transported, that you gaily fly;
Like Milton's chariot, that it lives—it feels—
And races from the spirit in the wheels.
  If mighty things with small we may compare
This spirit drives Britannia's conquering car,
Burns in her ranks—and kindles every Tar.
NELSON displayed its power upon the main,
And WELLINGTON exhibits it in Spain.
Another MARLBOROUGH points to Blenheim's story,

NOTES

And with its lústre blends his kindred glory.
   In Arms and Science long our Isle hath shone,
And SHAKSPEARE wondrous SHAKSPEARE—rear'd a
     throne
For British Poesy—whose powers inspire
The British pencil and the British lyre.
Her we invoke!—her sister Arts implore;
Their smiles beseech whose charms yourselves adore.
These, if we win, the Graces too we gain,—
Their dear belov'd, inseparable train;
Three who their witching airs from Cupid stole,
And three acknowledged sovereigns of the soul;
Harmonious throng! with nature blending art: ⎫
Divine Sestetto! warbling to the heart: ⎬
For Poesy shall here sustain the upper part. ⎭
Thus lifted, gloriously we'll sweep along,
Shine in our music, scenery and song:
Shine in our farce, masque opera and play,
And prove old Drury has not had her day.
Nay more—to stretch the wing, the world shall cry,
Old Drury never, never soared so high!
" But hold," you'll say, " this self-complacent boast:
Easy to reckon thus without your host."
True, true—that lowers at once our mounting pride:
'Tis yours alone our merit to decide;
'Tis ours to look to you—you hold the prize
That bids our great, our best ambition rise.
A double blessing your rewards impart
Each good provide, and elevate the heart,
Our twofold feeling owns its twofold cause:
Your bounty's comfort—rapture with applause;
When in your fostering beam you bid us live,
You give the means of life, and gild the means you give.

NOTES

This is Byron's Parody. (See *ante*, p. 10.)

PARENTHETICAL ADDRESS

by Dr. Plagiary

Half stolen, with acknowledgments, to be spoken in an inarticulate voice by Master P. at the opening of the next new theatre. Stolen parts marked with the inverted commas of quotation—thus "——".

" When energising objects men pursue,"
Then Lord knows what is writ by Lord knows who.
" A modest monologue you here survey "
Hiss'd from the theatre " the other day,"
As if Sir Fretful wrote " the slumberous " verse
And gave his son " the rubbish " to rehearse.
" Yet at the thing you'd never be amazed,"
Knew you the rumpus which the author raised;
" Nor even here your smile would be represt,"
Knew you these lines—the badness of the best.
" Flame! fire! and flame" (words borrowed from Lucretius)
" Dread metaphors which open wounds " like issues!
" And sleeping pangs awake—and—but away "
(Confound me if I know what next to say).
" So Hope reviving re-expands her wings "
And Master G. recites what Dr. Busby sings!—
" If mighty things with small we may compare,"
(Translated from the grammar for the fair!)
Dramatic " spirit drives a conquering car,"
And burned poor Moscow like a tub of " tar."
" This spirit Wellington has shown in Spain "
To furnish melodrames for Drury Lane.
" Another Marlborough points to Blenheim's story "
And George and I will dramatise it for ye.

NOTES

" In arts and sciences our isle hath shone "
(This deep discovery is mine alone).
" Oh British poesy, whose powers inspire "
My verse—or I'm a fool—and Fame's a liar,
" Thee we invoke, your sister arts implore "
With " smiles " and " lyres " and " pencils " and much
These, if we win the Graces, too, we gain   [more.
Disgraces, too! " inseparable train! "
" Three who have stolen their witching airs from
        Cupid "
(You all know what I mean unless you're stupid)
" Harmonious throng " that I have kept *in petto*
Now to produce in a " divine *sestetto* "!!
" While Poesy " with these delightful doxies,
" Sustains her part " in all the " upper " boxes!
" Thus lifted gloriously, you'll soar along,"
Borne in the vast balloon of Busby's song:
" Shine in your farce, masque, scenery and play "
(For this last line George had a holiday);
" Old Drury never, never soar'd so high,"
So says the manager, and so say I.
" But hold, you say, this self-complacent boast."
Is this the poem which the public lost?
" True—true—that lowers at once our mounting pride;"
But lo:—the papers print what you deride.
" 'Tis ours to look on you—you hold the prize,"
'Tis *twenty guineas* as they advertise!
" A double blessing your rewards impart "—
I wish I had them, then, with all my heart.
" Our *twofold* feeling *owns* its twofold cause,"
Why son and I both beg for your applause.
" When in your fostering beams you bid us live."
My next subscription list shall say how much you give.
            [Lord Byron]   October, 1812

NOTES

And the following is George Frederick's own effort:
Unalogue
by G. F. Busby, Esq.

Ye social energies that link mankind
In golden bands—as potent as refin'd!
That bid the precious tear of pity start,
Exalt the genius, purify the heart
Thrill with fine touch the chords of Campbell's lyre
Nerve Valour's arm and Wisdom's self inspire;
Guide Albion's force beyond the Southern main,
And plead so mightily for injur'd Spain;
Point each diviner impulse of the soul,
And work in individual for the whole—
Now be your power exerted—*Here* confest
Move in a British cause the British breast,
And hail your grandest triumph and your best;
They come, they come! above, below, around,
Soft voices breathe, and sweet responses sound:
Consenting murmurs melodize the air,
Thrill through my ravish'd breast, and echo there!
   Britons, your candid audience we beseech—
List to a Briton's plain but honest speech:
No Actor now laboriously essays
To rouse your passions, and extort your praise:
No mimic raptures teach your breasts to glow:
Such arts we scorn, superior ends demand
Superior means, and these we now command;
Keep Truth, keep Nature, full within our view—
And ónce do justice to ourselves, and—you.
Too long hath Native genius been obscur'd,
French *froth* and German *rant* too long endur'd:
Too long, a vicious appetite to pamper,
Britain's Thalia suffer Farce to cramp her

NOTES

Divine MELPOMENE a transient ray
Beam'd in *Alfonso* beam'd—and past away.
Then giddy Harlequin and senseless Clown
Rush'd forth; and bore all opposition down—
Rush'd grinning Pantaloon, and motley Fool,
Drove Sense away, and sway'd with mad mis-rule:
Burlesque and Melodrame usurp'd the Stage,
And wild monstrosity was all the rage!
Against these rude invaders now we make
A firm decisive stand for Britain's sake—
For Britain's sake—for shall the land that gave
A SHAKSPEARE birth, become the Drama's grave?
No! by his sacred Manes now we swear,
(And call on *you* the patriot task to share)
To root these rank abuses from our scene,
And show the world what England's stage hath been;
To bid *contemporary* genius shine,
Cast off his shroud, and reign by *right divine:*
Dare in *his* cause and *your's* stand forth *alone*
Mingle his sacred interests with our own,
Here fight his battle, and here fix his throne!
Thus, if with our's your breasts shall sympathize,
Shall other Shakspeares, Otways, Congreves rise;
Nature and Truth resume their ravish'd sway,
And Wit, exulting, hail the new born day.

36 Queen Ann-street West,
    Cavendish Square.

  James Smith's note is as follows: " Dr. Busby gave living recitations of his translation of *Lucretius*, with tea and bread-and-butter. He sent in a real Address to the Drury Lane Committee, which was really rejected. The present imitation professes to be recited by the translator's son. The poet here, again, was a prophet.

NOTES

A few evenings after the opening of the Theatre, Dr. Busby sat with his son in one of the stage-boxes. The latter, to the astonishment of the audience, at the end of the play, stepped from the box upon the stage, with his father's real rejected address in his hand, and began to recite it as follows:—

'When energising objects men pursue,
 What are the prodigies they cannot do?'

Raymond, the stage-manager, accompanied by a constable, at this moment walked upon the stage, and handed away the juvenile *dilettante* performer.

" The Doctor's classical translation was thus noticed in one of the newspapers of the day, in the column of births:—' Yesterday, at his house in Queen Anne-street, Dr. Busby of a still-born *Lucretius*." J. S.

The *Quarterly Review* wrote: " In one single point the parodist has failed—there is a certain Dr. Busby, whose supposed address is a translation called ' Architectural Atoms, intended to be recited by the translator's son.' Unluckily, however, for the wag who had prepared this fun, the *genuine serious absurdity* of Dr. Busby and his son has cast all his humour into the shade. The Doctor from the boxes, and the son from the stage, have actually endeavoured, it seems, to recite addresses, which they call *monologues* and *unalogues;* and which, for extravagant folly, tumid meanness, and vulgar affectation, set all the powers of parody at utter defiance."

Jeffrey, in the *Edinburgh Review*, said: " Of 'Architectural Atoms,' translated by Dr. Busby, we can say very little more than that they appear to us to be far more capable of combining into good poetry than the few lines we were able to read of the learned Doctor's genuine address in the newspapers. They might pass, indeed, for a very tolerable imitation of Darwin."

NOTES

NOTES

p. 98, *l.* 19. " Winsor's patent gas "—at that time in its infancy. The first place illumed by it was [Jan. 28, 1807] the Carlton-house side of Pall Mall; the second, Bishopsgate Street. The writer attended a lecture given by the inventor: the charge of admittance was three shillings, but, as the inventor was about to apply to parliament, members of both houses were admitted gratis. The writer and a fellow-jester assumed the parts of senators at a short notice. " Members of parliament! " was their important ejaculation at the door of entrance. " What places, gentlemen? " " Old Sarum and Bridgewater." " Walk in, gentlemen." Luckily, the real Simon Pures did not attend. This Pall Mall illumination was further noticed in *Horace in London*:—

" And Winsor lights, with flame of gas,
Home, to King's Place, his mother." J. S.

p. 101, *l.* 24. " Ticket-nights." This phrase is probably unintelligible to the untheatrical portion of the community, which may now be said to be all the world except the actors. Ticket-nights are those whereon the inferior actors club for a benefit: each distributes as many tickets of admission as he is able among his friends. A motley assemblage is the consequence; and, as each actor is encouraged by his own set, who are not in general play-going people, the applause comes (as Chesterfield says of Pope's attempt at wit) " generally unseasonably, and too often unsuccessfully." J. S.

XVI

THEATRICAL ALARM BELL. By the EDITOR of the MORNING POST

ACCORDING to Mr. Percy Fitzgerald, the writer intended here was Dr. Stoddart, a lawyer who wrote for the Press, commonly called Dr. Slop. Hazlitt married his sister.

NOTES

James Smith's note is as follows: " This journal was, at the period in question, rather remarkable for the use of the figure called by the rhetoricians *catachresis*. The Bard of Avon may be quoted in justification of its adoption, when he writes of taking arms against a sea, and seeking a bubble in the mouth of a cannon. The *Morning Post*, in the year 1812, congratulated its readers upon having stripped off Cobbett's mask and discovered his cloven foot; adding, that it was high time to give the hydra-head of Faction a rap on the knuckles! J. S.

XVII
THE THEATRE. By the Rev. GEORGE CRABBE

GEORGE CRABBE (1754-1832) was the sort of poet whose simplicity lent itself to parody. At the time when the parody was written everything of any value of Crabbe's, except *The Tales of the Hall*, had been written.

James Smith contributes the following note: "THE REV. GEORGE CRABBE.—The writer's first interview with this poet, who may be designated Pope in worsted stockings, took place at William Spencer's villa at Petersham, close to what that gentleman called his gold-fish pond, though it was scarcely three feet in diameter, throwing up a *jet d'eau* like a thread. The venerable bard, seizing both the hands of his satirist, exclaimed, with a good-humoured laugh, 'Ah! my old enemy, how do you do?' In the course of conversation, he expressed great astonishment at his popularity in London; adding, 'In my own village they think nothing of me.' The subject happening to be the inroads of time upon beauty, the writer quoted the following lines:—

NOTES

Six years had pass'd, and forty ere the six,
When Time began to play his usual tricks:
My locks, once comely in a virgin's sight,
Locks of pure brown, now felt th' encroaching white;
Gradual each day I liked my horses less,
My dinner more—I learnt to play at chess."

" ' That's very good! ' cried the bard;—' whose is it? ' ' Your own.' ' Indeed! hah! well, I had quite forgotten it.' Was this affectation, or was it not? In sooth, he seemed to push simplicity to puerility. This imitation contained in manuscript the following lines, after describing certain Sunday newspaper critics who were supposed to be present at a new play, and who were rather heated in their politics:—

' Hard is the task who edits—thankless job!—
A Sunday journal for the factious mob.
With bitter paragraph and caustic jest,
He gives to turbulence the day of rest;
Condemn'd, this week, rash rancour to instil,
Or thrown aside, the next, for one who will:
Alike undone or if he praise or rail
(For this affects his safety, that his sale),
He sinks at last, in luckless limbo set,
If loud for libel, and if dumb for debt.'[1]

" They were, however, never printed; being, on reflection, considered too serious for the occasion.

" It is not a little extraordinary that Crabbe, who could write with such vigour, should descend to such lines as the following:—

---

[1] Of these Moore wrote in his Diary that the last four lines were unequalled for neatness and execution.

NOTES

'Something had happen'd wrong about a bill
Which was not drawn with true mercantile skill;
So, to amend it, I was told to go
And seek the firm of Clutterbuck and Co.'

"Surely 'Emanuel Jennings,' compared with the above, rises to sublimity." J. S.

Jeffrey wrote in the *Edinburgh Review:* "'The Theatre,' by the Rev. G. Crabbe, we rather think, is the best piece in the collection. It is an exquisite and most masterly imitation, not only of the peculiar style, but of the taste, temper, and manner of description of that most original author; and can hardly be said to be in any respect a caricature of that style or manner—except in the excessive profusion of puns and verbal jingles—which, though undoubtedly to be ranked among his characteristics, are never so thick sown in his original works as in this admirable imitation. It does not aim, of course, at any shadow of his pathos or moral sublimity, but seems to us to be a singularly faithful copy of his passages of mere description."

Someone had written to Crabbe condoling with him on the parody, to which he replied: "You were more feeling than I was, when you read the excellent parodies of the young men who wrote the 'Rejected Addresses.' There is a little ill-nature—and I take the liberty of adding, undeserved ill-nature—in their prefatory address; but in their versification they have done me admirably. They are extraordinary men; but it is easier to imitate style than to furnish matter" (*Works*, 1 vol. ed., p. 81).

NOTES

XVIII, XIX, XX
MACBETH TRAVESTIE, etc.

THESE three parodies of George Colman were unworthy of the book, and were clearly only admitted in desperation. This class of song had already been represented in No. XIV, " Drury's Husting."

Jeffrey wrote of them in the *Edinburgh Review:* " We come next to three ludicrous parodies—of the story of *The Stranger*, of *George Barnwell*, and of the dagger-scene in *Macbeth*, under the signature of Momus Medlar. They are as good, we think, as that sort of thing can be, and remind us of the happier efforts of Colman, whose less successful fooleries are professedly copied in the last piece in the volume."

XXI
PUNCH'S APOTHEOSIS. By THEODORE HOOK
(1788-1841)

JAMES SMITHS'S note says: " Theodore Hook, at that time a very young man, and the companion of the annotator in many wild frolics. The cleverness of his subsequent prose compositions has cast his early stage songs into oblivion. This parody was, in the second edition, transferred from Colman to Hook."

The reason for the transfer is not clear. Colman may have objected, but more probably Hook wanted to be admitted and Colman was already taken off in the previous travesties.

NOTES

p. 125, *l*. 14. Then Director of the Opera House. J. S.

p. 125, *l*. 15. At that time the chief dancer at this establishment. J. S.

p. 126, *l*. 13. Vauxhall Bridge then, like the Thames Tunnel at present, stood suspended in the middle of that river. J.S.

Jeffrey writes in the *Edinburgh Review:* " ' Punch's Apotheosis,' by G. Colman, junior, is too purely nonsensical to be extracted; and both gives less pleasure to the reader, and does less justice to the ingenious author in whose name it stands, than any other of the poetical imitations."

BIBLIOGRAPHY

THE First Edition of the *Rejected Addresses* has indications of the haste in which it was produced. The Second Edition was carefully revised and shows many alterations. This text was thereafter maintained practically unchanged—there being in the Seventeenth and Eighteenth Editions only a few minor verbal changes. The text here followed is that of the Eighteenth Edition, the last to which the brothers Smith can be said to have given any attention. Variations from the First Edition are noted below; unless otherwise stated the changes were made in the Second Edition.

PREFACE. *In First Edition.*

p. 18, *l.* 7, *after* " that Address has been preserved " *read* " and was thought worthy of taking the lead," *instead of* " and in the ensuing pages takes the lead."

p. 18, *l.* 30, *instead of* " the Editor does " *read* " we do"; at *l.* 32 *for* " he is " *read* " we are;" and *p.* 19, *ll.* 6 and 7 *for* " he has " *read* " we have."

CONTENTS, *p.* 33. *In First Edition.*

No. III, *An Address without a Phœnix*, was at No. XVI, *Cui Bono?* being No. III. *The Theatre* was No. XX, and XXI, *Punch's Apotheosis*, was attributed to G[eorge] C[olman] the Younger.

No. IV. CUI BONO? By Lord B. *In First Edition.*

Stanza II, *l.* 2, *read* " To gaze on dupes who meet an equal doom."

Stanza IX, *l.* 8, *read* " Ye all shall wail in poverty your wrong."

Stanza X, *l.* 1, *read* " So fares the bard who sings in fashion's train."

Stanza X, *l.* 4, *read* " Then round his skeleton wind laurel wreath."

Stanza X, l. 5, *for* " empty " *read* " balmy."
Stanza X, l. 9, *for* " trampling " *read* " trample."
Stanza XI, l. 9, *for* " stable yard " *read* " four-in-hand."

No. V. HAMPSHIRE FARMER'S ADDRESS. *In First Edition.*

p. 53, *l.* 19, *for* " to boot! " *read* " too."
p. 54, *l.* 1, *for* " to use as rammers for paving " *read* " to break into pebbles to pave."
p. 55, *l.* 4, *omit* " mind I don't vouch for the fact, but I am told—you will find."

No. VI. THE LIVING LUSTRES. *In First Edition.*
Stanzas IV to VII read as follows:

IV

Each pillar that opens our stage to the circle is
Verdant antique like Ninon de l'Enclos;
I'd ramble from them to the pillars of Hercules
Give me but Rosa wherever I go.

V

Same as IV in this edition, but *l.* 1 *for* " actors " *read* " artists."

VI

Attuned to the scene when the pale yellow moon is on
Tower and tree they'd look sober and sage,
And when they'd all wink their dear peepers in unison
Night, pitchy night would envelop the stage.

VII

Ah could I some girl from yon box for her youth pick
I'd love her as long as she blossomed in youth;
Oh! white is the ivory case of the tooth pick
But when beauty smiles how much whiter the tooth!

Stanza IX, l. 4, *read* " Which watered in crimson encircle their brows."
Stanza VIII, l. 1, *for* " For " *read* "And."

No. VII. THE REBUILDING. *In First Edition.*

p. 59, *l.* 10, *read* " *The* tops of houses."
p. 60, *l.* 18, *for* " run " *read* " flock."
p. 60, *l.* 19, *for* " Sun " *read* " Rock."
p. 60, *l.* 30, *for* " bellow " *read* " hollow."

BIBLIOGRAPHY

p. 61, *l.* 8, *for* " workmen " *read* " firemen."

p. 62, *l.* 32, *for* " winged " *read* " urged " (*changed in Seventeenth Edition*).

p. 63, *omit l.* 22 " Wakes from their humid caves, the sleeping Nine " (*this was not added until Seventeenth Edition*).

p. 64, *omit l.* 29 " Whizzing aloft, like the Temple fountain."

p. 65, *l.* 20, *omit—*
    Soon as thy maiden sister Di.
    Caps with her copper lid the dark blue sky,
    And through the fissures of her clouded fan
    Peeps at the naughty monster man.
(*Added in the Eighteenth Edition.*)

No. IX. A TALE OF DRURY LANE. *In First Edition.*

p. 72, *l.* 16, *for* ' red " *read* " the " (*changed in Seventeenth Edition*).

p. 73, *l.* 19, *for* The Hand in Hand the race begun
    Then came the Phœnix and the Sun.
  read The Sun the London and the Rock
    The Pelican which nought can shock.

No. X. JOHNSON'S GHOST. *In First Edition.*

p. 81, *l.* 9, *for* " conclusively reply " *read* " frame a response."

No. XI. THE BEAUTIFUL INCENDIARY. *In First Edition.*
Stanza X, *l.* 8, *read* " Me and Lady Elizabeth Mugg."

No. XV. ARCHITECTURAL ATOMS. *In First Edition.*

p. 99, *l.* 4, *for* " sable " *read* " jetty " (*changed in Eighteenth Edition*).

p. 99, *omit ll.* 21 and 22, " Fools . . . mine."

p. 99, *l.* 23, *for* " Each sly Sangrado, with his poisonous pen " *read* " Each, pen in hand, with literary skill."

p. 99, *l.* 29, *for—*
    Where Day and Martin's patent blacking roll'd,
    Burst from the vase Pactolian streams of gold.
      read—
    Where blacking poured its sooty tide behold
    Glad Day and Martin's sail in stream of gold.

BIBLIOGRAPHY

p. 100, *l.* 2, *for* " Win annual tribute by the annual lie! " *read* " Mount the tall wheels and coin the annual lie."

p. 101, *omit ll.* 16 and 17 " So . . . await; "

p. 101, *omit ll.* 23 and 24 " Some . . . make: "

p. 101, *l.* 26, *for* " strangled " *read* " murdered."

p. 102, *l.* 9, *for* " beauties " *read* " lovers."

p. 102, *l.* 19, *for*—
But of unhallow'd fascinations sick
Soon quits his Cyprian for his married brick;
read—
But soon resigns the tie appall'd and sick
He quits the Cyprian for his married brick.

p. 103, *l.* 15, *for* "Back to the base resulting with a bound" *read* " Back to the bottom leaping with a bound " (*changed in Eighteenth Edition*).

p. 103, *l.* 19, *for* " On trudged the Gemini to reach the rail " *read* " Their spread and balanced fingers touch the rail."

No. XVI. THEATRICAL ALARM BELL. *In First Edition.*

p. 106, *l.* 3, *for* " Thursday " *read* " Friday."

No. XVII. THE THEATRE. *In First Edition.*

p. 114, *omit ll.* 15-18 " John Richard . . . shoes."

p. 115, *omit ll.* 7-8 " Or till . . . eight? " (*inserted in Fourteenth Edition*).

p. 115, *l.* 15, *for* " clue " *read* " hue " (*changed in Seventeenth Edition*).

No. XVIII. MACBETH TRAVESTIE. *In First Edition.*

p. 116, *l.* 12, *for* " very " *read* " most."

p. 117, *l.* 11, *for* " add's " *read* "odd's" (*changed in Seventeenth Edition*).

No. XXI. PUNCH'S APOTHEOSIS. *In First Edition.*

p. 126, *l.* 18, *for* " One loves long gloves " *read* " I love a long glove."

The *First Edition* is a 12mo consisting of half-title, title, Preface p. iv-xiii, xiv blank, xv list of Contents, xvi blank, text 1-126, 127 has publisher's advt., 128 blank, imprint at foot of 126.

BIBLIOGRAPHY

The title-page runs: Rejected Addresses:/or/The New/Theatrum Poetarum/[rule]" Fired that the House reject him—'Sdeath! I'll *print* it/"And Shame the Fools." Pope [rule] London:/Printed for John Miller, 25, Bow Street/Covent Garden./[rule] 1812.

Bound in blue-grey or buff boards with paper label. " Rejected/Addresses/4/6./Published Monday, Oct. 12th, 1812.

The *Second Edition* was considerably altered: the text runs on to p. 127 which has the imprint, 128 is blank. No further changes were made in subsequent editions. The *Thirteenth Edition* (1813) is large paper (demy 8vo size), evidently for the purpose of extra illustration. Some editions were printed by Ballantyne and have Constable's imprint. The *Sixteenth Edition* was printed by Ballantyne, but had a cancel title with Gale and Polden as publishers, indicating that Miller had sold it. Murray—who bought it (see pp. 26 and 32) —must have bought it from them. His first edition, *the Seventeenth Edition*, was sm. cr. 8vo, 1819. To the *Eighteenth Edition* Horace wrote the Preface and James contributed the Notes, and Cruikshank six woodcuts. The tinted portrait of the brothers Smith, by Harlowe, first appears there. This edition is sm. cr. 8vo (often miscalled 12mo). The numeration is misleading, indicating that there should have been a half-title. The collation, however, does not call for it. In the next edition there is one. To the *Twenty-second* Edition (1851) Mr. Peter Cunningham contributed an Advertisement (about the brothers Smith) and some notes. In 1890 Mr. Percy Fitzgerald edited an edition for Messrs. Pickering and Chatto, with some interesting notes and a useful Introduction.

As for the actual manuscripts of the genuine Rejected

BIBLIOGRAPHY

Addresses, they (including Horace Smith's own contribution) fell by some chance into the hands of a Mr. Winston, who had them mounted into two 4to volumes. They were sold among his books in 1849, and twelve years later figure in a catalogue of Messrs. Wells and Sotheran at a price of £8 10s.; and are now to be found in the MS. Room at the British Museum.